It Was Nice To Meet Me Again

Life-Changing Pandemic Insights and Adventures

Silvana Graf

"It Was Nice To Meet Me Again"

Copyright © 2022 Silvana Graf, all rights reserved.

No part of this publication may be reproduced, distributed,
or transmitted in any form or by any means,
including photocopying, recording, or any other electronic
or mechanical methods, without written consent by the author,
except in the case of brief quotations embodied in reviews and
other non-commercial uses permitted by international copyright laws.

ISBN No. 978-0-578-35631-0

BISAC: BIO026000   BIOGRAPHY & AUTOBIOGRAPHY / Personal Memoirs

Contents

Preface
page 5

Introduction
page 7

CHAPTER 1 · My Mother's 90th Birthday and a Goodbye to Gatherings, Hugs, and Kisses
page 11

CHAPTER 2 · Meditation for Becoming my Own Best Friend
page 23

CHAPTER 3 · Meeting Happiness
page 31

CHAPTER 4 · Equestrian Love and The Enchanted House on the Hill
page 39

CHAPTER 5 · Practicing Yoga for Grounding the Mind
page 53

CHAPTER 6 · Mindful Thursday Zoom
page 57

CHAPTER 7 · Connecting with People Far Away but Close to my Heart
page 63

CHAPTER 8 · Lavender Power
page 71

CHAPTER 9 · The Forest is my Church
page 75

CHAPTER 10 · Swimming in the Lake
page 83

CHAPTER 11 · The River
page 85

CHAPTER 12 · Returning to Lake Huron
page 91

CHAPTER 13 · Adopting Río, The Happy Tripod
page 95

CHAPTER 14 · Rediscovering Music
page 103

CHAPTER 15 · Photography of Life
page 107

CHAPTER 16 · Befriending Death
page 111

Final Words
page 115

Acknowledgements
page 117

To my True Self and the Web of Life I belong to. I am listening.

It Was Nice To Meet Me Again

Life-Changing Pandemic Insights and Adventures

Preface

What do you do when faced with a situation you have no power over? Do you resist, struggle, and let fear permeate your life? Or do you fully accept the limitations life presents and make the best of them?

On March 13, 2020, I decided that I would not let a virus lead me into depression. Instead, I would use the global health crisis as an opportunity for inner growth. I was ready to receive the lessons as they presented themselves and embrace the "isness" of life with neutrality and curiosity. Any difficulty will always be the best teacher if we are open to learning without resistance.

This book is my humble attempt at explaining some introspection work and the actions I took to maintain my sanity and even thrive spiritually during the unprecedented COVID-19 pandemic. I hope my journey can benefit others. I do acknowledge my privileged situation. I have deep empathy for the hardships others have endured while I had the positive experiences I describe in this book.

I wish that by the time you end this book, dear reader, my journey can help you make the best of a difficult situation. Throughout the pages of this book, I will show you how I learned to be kind to myself and honor my true self. Your essential self is always there, accessible to you, as a source of peace and love. Once you learn to fully accept and cherish yourself as if you were a newborn baby, there is an unlimited supply of love to share with the world.

It Was Nice To Meet Me Again

I will place as a backdrop the memories of my trip to Peru for my mother's 90th birthday three weeks before the United States government declared COVID-19 a National Emergency (3/13/2020). The purpose of this part of my story is to establish a contrast with what was about to happen to our world. Those drastic changes were painful but also created opportunities for me. I will also describe memories of my childhood, teenage years, and young adulthood as they relate to the experiences I lived through during the health crisis.

To open doors and windows into my inner self and stay healthy and positive, these are the most important choices I made:

- I learned to become a frequent meditator.
- I stopped trying to meet other peoples' expectations.
- I became my own best friend.
- I listened to my inner child and nurtured her.
- I chose to be physically active in nature.
- I practiced yoga and danced like no one was looking.
- I watched the news only sporadically to avoid the tsunami of negativity.
- I communicated with family and friends through internet applications.
- I reignited my connection to animals in the countryside.
- I organized outdoor activities with friends.
- I photographed details of my outdoor adventures.
- I focused on what unites me with my fellow human beings.
- I created space for music in my life.
- I befriended Death.
- I wrote this book.

It was through this journey that I was able to find my true self again.

Introduction

When the COVID-19 pandemic started hitting the news, I had already been warned about its likely severity by my brother Flavio, who is an expert at predicting calamities. I don't know if it's a psychic gift, a result of devoting significant time to researching things ahead of most people, or both! While my family laughs sometimes and calls him "The Doom and Gloom," I pay attention just in case... If what he communicates makes sense to me, I find it sensible to take practical precautions. At the same time, I'm not dragged into fear by his views.

In general, my survival instincts have always been intense. I am not the risk-taker type. I don't like roller coasters or white-water rafting. After giving birth to Stefan in 1992, I developed a very conscious sense of responsibility to stay alive. I remember telling myself, "Darn it, now I can't die in peace!" Then I had Mattias in 1997, and that feeling became even more accentuated. However, this protective motherly feeling did not mean that I would not enjoy the outdoors. As a family, our love of nature has been the thread that connects us at a deeper level. So, I tried not to obsess about safety and I let my husband teach the kids to become "wild goats." At the same time, I was pretty careful and clung to dear life.

In the context of the pandemic, I adopted the early use of the mask. I avoided physically going to the grocery store, especially before it became mandatory to use a mask in indoor settings in Michigan. When everyone started wearing a face covering, I would go to the stores during non-peak hours without hesitation. I was the first of my friends to organize a backyard gathering. We kept our 6 feet social distance, wore masks, and used hand sanitizer before touching anything. That was sometime in June 2020. It was lovely to see friends again! Each of the six guests expressed how happy they were chatting with friends after months of social isolation. Thereafter, once a month or so, others started organizing

It Was Nice To Meet Me Again

small get-togethers, but for the most part, we spent our free time within our households. There was much we did not know about how the virus spread, and there were a lot of mixed messages in the official government channels.

Now that my kids are adults and don't need me to survive, Death has become my friend. It is not a subject I avoid; it reminds me of impermanence; it helps me appreciate every moment. I can look Death in the eye. I am not afraid of it. Meditating about it helps me live more fully and "not sweat the small stuff!"

I hope to arrive at the feet of Death consciously. It will be "the ultimate and deepest meditation of all." I will let go of attachments. I will be free to reunite with the One Universal Spirit that permeates all existence. I genuinely feel we are only like waves that temporarily manifest as individuals with unique characteristics to later blend in with the sea again and be peace itself. Both my head and heart accept this humble view of the circle of life.

For now, while fully alive, mindfulness guides me. During the last 15 years, I've had several amazing teachers (Jon Kabat-Zinn, Eckhart Tolle, Pema Chodron, Thich Nhat Hanh, Jack Kornfield, Rick Hanson, and most recently, Alejandra Llamas, Sarah Blondin, and others from the Insight Timer Community). Thanks to them, my mindful friends, and my natural intuition, I have been able to navigate the COVID-19 health crisis and my family's challenges as learning opportunities. It has been a space for self-rediscovery and inner growth.

Publishing my first book has been the fulfillment of a lifelong dream. It's never too late, and I will continue writing until the end of my days. It may become apparent as you read, but English is not my first language, and it's not the only language I use daily. My brain switches from English to Spanish, and vice versa, many times during the day. But for some reason, I needed to write this journey in the language in which I first learned about mindfulness.

Just as a funny note, in 1986, a few months after I arrived in Madison, my now-husband Rolf and his dad invited me to a fancy steakhouse. I ordered a "medium-raw T-bone steak with smashed potatoes." I will never have that difficulty again as I'm now a vegetarian (ha, ha). But regardless of that, I hope several decades later, I don't make mistakes of that sort. If I do, just laugh, please. You will understand anyway, like the kind waiter at that restaurant.

Photo Credit: Stefan Petrmichl, ashtewan.com

Chapter 1
My Mother's 90th Birthday and a Goodbye to Gatherings, Hugs and Kisses

Lucha Málaga "The Great" turned 90 on March 3rd, 2020. We started planning for the special celebration about eight months ahead of time. Several close family members are spread out worldwide, so we had to plan the logistics of organizing some aspects of the celebration from a distance and then getting to Lima, Peru, in time.

Early in January, my brother Flavio started talking about canceling the family trip to Peru. No one else was predicting frontier closings yet, but he was, and he seemed obsessed with it. Flavio and his family live in Switzerland and Flavio was afraid of catching the virus and not being able to re-enter Switzerland if things got bad. Some of Flavio's family members were legal residents but not citizens yet, and that could make a difference given Switzerland's strict immigration policies. There were many unknowns.

I implored Flavio not to cancel the trip because it was important to my mom. She had been looking forward to seeing her family together on this day for many months. But Flavio was hesitant even as he, his wife Paola, and his children Lara and Emil boarded that plane.

In retrospect, my brother and I were both right. Things did get bad eventually; some borders around the world closed. We, however, had enough time to celebrate my mother's life and show her our love in person, before we couldn't anymore.

In mid-February of 2020, according to plan, I boarded a plane from Detroit to Lima. Following Flavio's advice, I traveled with an

It Was Nice To Meet Me Again

N95 mask. I was the only person on board wearing a mask. It felt odd, but the last thing I wanted was to infect my elderly parents upon arrival. I took disinfectant wipes with me and cleaned the surfaces around my seat. I was cautious.

I arrived in Lima to find long lines at the airport waiting to go through immigration and I felt nervous about being in a crowded space. I spotted a few travelers arriving from other parts of the world wearing masks, probably feeling the same way.

For my mother's birthday celebration, we invited close family, some extended family members, and my mother's friends (primarily elderly women, card sharks among them!). The setting was a beautiful beach house with a magnificent view of the ocean. We had a rainbow of stunning flowers decorating every available surface and a lovely buffet cooked by a talented chef, my cousin Sari. She made gourmet hors d'oeuvres, exquisite Peruvian sea bass, seafood dishes, pork, and plenty of vegetarian dishes such as quinoa, fried yucca with Huancaína sauce, and fava bean salad. Both Flavio and I are vegetarians – still somewhat unusual in Peru – and Sari made sure we had plenty to eat.

My mom has trouble walking and her vision is fading. She was born with a deformed hip, and later in life, developed macular degeneration. A hip replacement 30 years ago in Chile did wonders, but nothing lasts forever. I would have to write another book to give proper justice to Lucha's unique and dramatic life. A Netflix series in the making!

Before the celebration, my brother Flavio instructed his kids to wash their faces and hands thoroughly whenever guests kissed them and, in any case, to avoid such situations when possible. After he meticulously demonstrated the precise procedure, my niece and nephew kept running to the bathroom to comply with these fatherly orders. Poor things. At that time, the pandemic was perceived as a problem in faraway China that could not possibly spread to Peru! And so it was hard to avoid hugs and kisses without offending the guests. It's incredible how fast things changed; five days later, the government announced the first case of Covid-19 in Peru.

My Mother's 90th Birthday and a Goodbye to Gatherings, Hugs and Kisses
Silvana Graf

At her party, my Mami was happy and beautiful. She gracefully chose her clothes, as she always does. The night before the party, Luchita slept in curlers; in the morning, she sat in front of her magnifying mirror and put on her makeup. This is a special ritual for her; it relaxes her, and the results are always impressive. Her makeup session is as close as it gets to a "meditation" in my mother's world. She can't see much, but thanks to years of practice, she remembers the shape of her eyebrows, eyelids, and sensual lips. Nobody can believe her age. That day she was radiant like royalty – inside and out.

There were a little over forty guests. The planned entertainment featured a band of musicians who played my mom's favorite boleros. After that, mariachis came to sing "Las Mañanitas" from below the terrace, and we all sang along to other beautiful songs. A curious contextual note is that the mariachis were not Mexican or Peruvian. The musicians were talented Venezuelans running away from the chaos of the Maduro regimen.

Some of us stood up and danced around when the Mariachis came up the stairs and into the living room. I asked one of my favorite uncles, Daniel Málaga, to give me the honor of dancing with him. He had been very ill the year before; many thought we would lose him. But he recovered and had not danced in ages. Well, I asked him to dance with me and he did it with enthusiasm and good rhythm. The elderly are precious beings who have not retired from living. The greatest gift younger people who surround them can provide is to give them opportunities to express the many aspects of their being. It was great for tío Daniel to know he could still dance, and I loved it too.

Uncle Daniel is most knowledgeable and entertaining. He makes me laugh and has a wealth of information regarding the family's history. He recently informed us that "Abra Málaga," a high mountain pass in the Andes of Peru, is where our Spanish ancestors, who were muleteers, came through on horses at some point in history. I don't know if it's true, but it sure sounds fascinating. My uncle is a man of faith without "intermediaries," as he says. His relationship with God does not involve a church or any preachers. Peru is a

It Was Nice To Meet Me Again

predominantly Catholic country, and tío Daniel irreverently excels at pointing out contradictions within the Catholic Church. For instance, he told us that several Málaga descendants were children of a promiscuous highland Catholic bishop called Pablo, who never wanted to be a priest in the first place. Tío Daniel is a rebel in his generation.

At one point, the music stopped suddenly, and Isaías Vivas, the leader of the mariachis, asked the family to say a few words to honor the birthday girl. None of us had prepared for this, but I volunteered to go first. I looked within and found words that reflected my profound gratitude to my mom for having taught me to appreciate life. My mom would always say, "Mira qué lindo, hijita" ("look how beautiful, my daughter"). She pointed at the flowers, trees, birds, and every detail of nature. She taught me to be curious and explore the world beyond any frontier. Her prompts to look around could get annoying at times, but it worked; she trained my mind and my eyes to SEE. As a mother, I did the same with my kids. I am sure I annoyed them at times, but something stuck. That attention to detail, combined with my dad's photography hobby, led me to become an avid photographer of nature, people, and structures. Now my son Stefan follows in our footsteps as well.

Flavio expressed his gratitude by saying that my mother taught him to be a warrior and never give up. "La Gran Lucha" ("Lucha the Great") was always there for him, like a rock he could lean against when he needed her. Flavio took time to mature and find his North, but my mother never gave up on him. Her support led him to get an MBA at Cranfield University, England. That step was fundamental in opening doors for him in Europe to develop a successful career in Spain and later Switzerland.

My older brother Gonzalo, who lives in Lima, said he could not speak because he would get too emotional, and to please excuse him. What he did not say, but I know he believes, is that my mother is a determined woman with great common sense and drive despite not having a college education. Because of her encouragement and support Gonzalo was awarded a Fullbright scholarship to study engineering in the United States. He was a gifted, hardworking

My Mother's 90th Birthday and a Goodbye to Gatherings, Hugs and Kisses
Silvana Graf

17-year-old who obtained a bachelor's degree at the University of Arkansas and a master's degree at Stanford University before turning 21. He became the youngest engineer to ever work at IBM in Peru. My mom's excellent advice led to my brother's success as an adult. In turn, Gonzalo's example motivated me to apply for a scholarship at the University of Wisconsin in 1985. As a result, later on, I obtained a master's in Environmental Law and Policy. That decision also changed my life.

My mother's good example had a lasting positive effect on our lives. She pushed us to explore the world beyond our comfort zone at the cost of getting separated from her. She wanted the best for us without any regard for the consequences for her.

The absence at the reunion of my late sister, Ani, was deeply felt but not mentioned. We did not want my mom to get sad. Ani sadly passed away on July 2nd, 2018, from metastatic breast cancer at the age of 67. She was my mom's companion. It was devastating for my mom, but as my mom's nickname is "Lucha" ("fight"), she keeps fighting for her life despite her emotional and physical difficulties.

With her elegance and attention to detail, Ani would have loved to be there on such a special occasion. I could envision her with a beautiful light beige linen outfit and a necklace made of shells with matching earrings. She would have arranged the flowers most artistically and made sure every pillow in the room was leaning at the right angle on each sofa. Instead, her best sis-friend, Sabine Ledgard, was to celebrate my mom's life.

During my sister's last days on this Earth, I adopted Sabine as my sis-friend. We both loved my sister unconditionally and were there together until the end. I was delighted that she could attend my mother's celebration. You know, it is possible to inherit best friends; I did it. Ani unites us in spirit forever.

My uncle Tomás also wanted to dedicate some heartfelt words to my mom. He was so moved by the whole celebration that he could not speak Spanish, his native tongue. He has lived most of his adulthood in Brazil, and the meaningful words of gratitude for

It Was Nice To Meet Me Again

my mom came out in Portuguese mixed with tears. We understood anyway and cried with him. He said that my mother's unconditional help and support during critical moments of his journey changed his destiny completely. Lucha was there when he needed her most in his professional career. She is a wonderful sister, he said.

Tomás took the time to design a book with the lyrics of my mom's favorite boleros, in large font (for the elderly) and intertwined with old-time pictures of my beautiful mother. He made copies for the participants. Luchita has a beautiful voice; she could have been a singer. She sang her children and grandchildren to sleep with a song called "Muñequita(o) Linda(o)," (Pretty Little Doll.) It still gives me shivers, especially the time she sang for my sister on her last day. The band played that song, and it was very emotional.

There were many teary eyes during this celebration. It was extraordinary and a source of beautiful memories that kept my mom going through the prolonged worldwide health crisis. The momentous party has since been a big subject of conversation amongst everyone who was there. Her friends enjoyed it very much and will never forget it either.

For me, Lucha's 90th birthday was a very emotional trip to my roots. I have lived in the United States of America since I won a scholarship to study for a Master's in Legal Institutions (Environmental Law and Policy) at the University of Wisconsin-Madison in 1986. I am 59 years old as I write this book. Thirty-five years in the U.S. represents "most of my life" at this point. Even though I go to Peru every year, there are some friends of my mom I have not seen for many years. On this occasion, I saw people who were integral to my childhood memories in Peru. Seeing and hugging those elderly ladies, whose faces were familiar to me despite the obvious passage of time, was an incredible gift. I felt their love in my bones, and I love them back.

During that afternoon, one of my mom's best friends needed to go to the restroom; she was frail under the weight of age; she needed my help to get to the bathroom and asked me to go inside with her like you would ask only a daughter. When I was a child, this woman watched me play with her daughter, so I was happy to do it. I admire people who can accept when they need help and don't feel it is beyond their dignity to ask and receive. It takes courage to show your vulnerabilities. As I once heard, "Getting old ain't for the faint of heart."(Anthony Hopkins)

Other friends of my mom, several younger than her but still elderly, surprised me with their vitality. One of them, called Susana Molina, is originally from Arequipa, where my mother grew up. She is one of my favorite "aunties"(not of blood). I remember her vividly as being knowledgeable about the politics of the '70s and '80s. She was the bright, witty, sexy lady with the low-cut dresses. Men and women turned their heads when she arrived in her latest and most spectacular outfits at the many parties my parents held at our house in Chacarilla del Estanque. Unlike other women in that era, she delighted in talking to men about the economy. Other women mostly gathered together and talked about their travels, country club gossip, and problems with their maids. Susana was captivating.

Well, in March 2020, Susana was as funny and charming as ever. Her wit, glamor, and deep cleavage had survived the passage of time. After many years (probably 25 or more), I sincerely enjoyed seeing her again. I have heard she has a lovely Bed & Breakfast in San Isidro, a classy neighborhood in Lima. I can imagine her welcoming and charming the foreign tourists! I wonder if she had to change her business model with the pandemic. It has been hard for the tourism and hospitality business.

The celebration of life that started this chapter is now a cherished memory, and much has changed. Thankfully, none of us got Covid as a result of the birthday party, and we had a memorable birthday celebration. At that time, we could not have imagined that it would be the last gathering of that type in Peru for two years and counting. The way things developed for everyone worldwide made the reunion even more significant than imagined. Several of my mother's friends who attended her birthday party have deeply felt the virus-imposed social isolation. Some fell into depression and one died.

It Was Nice To Meet Me Again

In the spring of 2020, for humanity as a whole, physical expressions of friendliness, closeness, and love became something to fear. Birthdays, weddings, graduations, religious gatherings, celebrations, or meetings of any kind were forbidden or strongly discouraged in their usual physical form. Spontaneous human connection was taken away from us. We had to reinvent our habits, culture, and expressions of love. The lucky ones had the resources and ability to use technology. Those of us who could learn to "Zoom," "Google-meet," "Skype," and "WhatsApp" our hugs and kisses. For the poor and disadvantaged of the world, it's been a very different story, and I am only attempting to tell the experience I lived through.

Vaccination was a slow process in Peru initially due to the political turmoil and instability. After a long period of economic growth and successive democratic governments (not without its share of corruption), political instability started when President Pedro Pablo Kuczynski resigned over allegations of corruption. He was replaced by his vice-president Manuel Vizcarra, who was later forced to relinquish the presidency over allegations of crime. Francisco Sagasti, a very respected member of Congress, replaced Vizcarra and he was able to start a vigorous vaccination campaign. His interim presidency lasted 8 months until new elections took place.

Marxist-Leninist President Pedro Castillo was elected by a sliver in a second-round election. The center and right-wing parties divided the free-market-economy vote (Too many wanted to be presidents.). So in the end, the two worst options ran against each other, Keiko Fujimori and Pedro Castillo, the second being the most unprepared president in the history of Peru. All this happened in a matter of two years.

The logistics of immunization and testing felt like a slow process for the people of the United States as well but not as bad as in Peru. Older people were prioritized due to their higher risk of dying of COVID-19. Being 58 at the time, I received my first Moderna vaccine on March 18, 2021, and the second vaccine on April 15, 2021, both

My Mother's 90th Birthday and a Goodbye to Gatherings, Hugs and Kisses
Silvana Graf

in Michigan. I remember feeling thrilled to have received my shots. After getting the second shot, I had a slight fever, joint aches, and felt very tired. But on May 4th, 2021, I left for Peru after more than a year of not being able to visit my parents.

I missed my mother's 91st birthday (in person), but we had a family Zoom session that day. In the end, the celebration was much nicer than she had imagined. The virtual meeting was well-attended by her siblings and nieces from all over the world. Her sister Isabel showed up at her apartment with the best chocolate cake in Lima. Her children and grandchildren had ordered flowers through WhatsApp (free international communications), widely used among Latin-Americans. And my brother later came to see her with his partner Lorena and brought another delicious birthday cake. So, she felt very celebrated despite COVID-19.

It has been an interesting process. Celebrations are not the same as before the virus, but there is always a way to make someone feel special wherever there is love and intention. Technology has become crucial to allow expressions of love, music, art, and creativity to continue, even if in a different format. Education had to change to internet learning. Not much could be the same way during the pandemic, in terms of human interactions, and only those willing or able to adapt thrived. Many creative celebrations have taken place internationally, such as car caravans and parades to honor a birthday person, a new graduate, or just to honor being alive. Opera singers have been singing from windows and balconies. Musicians, in increasing numbers, have been playing in the streets or below windows "mariachi-style" in more densely populated areas. Tips were received with gratitude

For the poor of the world, the choice to adapt to technology did not exist. The inequality gap became wider with the worldwide health crisis, and there will be lasting consequences both on the educational and economic fronts. The poor, as always, disproportionately suffer during epidemics and natural disasters.

In the case of Peru, the despair caused by the health crisis, despite significant efforts to contain it, has led to the election of

It Was Nice To Meet Me Again

an old-fashioned Marxist-Leninist President, Pedro Castillo. He represents a complete shift away from the market economy that has allowed Peru to grow steadily for the last forty years.

I mention these socio-economic and political aspects of the pandemic in Peru because I am very aware of the privileged position of this Peruvian-American woman writing this book in the beautiful college town of Ann Arbor, Michigan, in the United States of America. A place where the pandemic did not prevent me from walking in my neighborhood streets or local nature reserves.

My Mother's 90th Birthday and a Goodbye to Gatherings, Hugs and Kisses
Silvana Graf

Insights

- Celebrate yourself and your loved ones when you can, don't take anything for granted.
- When it's safe, express your love to your family and friends with hugs and kisses; you don't know when the last time will be.
- Tell, your loved ones, how grateful you are to have them in your life.
- Appreciate the elderly and honor them.
- Accept and adapt to change, there is no point in resisting.
- Focus on what you can do; move forward.

It Was Nice To Meet Me Again

Chapter 2

Meditation for Becoming my Own Best Friend

The COVID-19 lockdown started in Michigan on March 24, 2020. After that day, I did not have to drive every other day before sunrise to avoid traffic from Ann Arbor to Southfield. Working 100% from home was an opportunity to create a new morning routine. Steve, the Managing Director in the commercial real estate company I worked for, had given us a 66-day-challenge intended to create a work/productivity-related habit change. He claimed that human behavioral research indicated that 66 days of doing something makes a new pattern, and he suggested we create a new positive habit. I decided that keeping a consistent meditation practice would help me stay positive during the testing times of COVID-19. That was a solid base for anything else I wanted to achieve.

I took the plunge. I printed the 66-day form, stuck it to a prominent wall in the kitchen area, and made my first X-cross on day 1. I also announced my decision to my close friends and family, posting it on Facebook. I wanted to be held accountable by the world. One day at a time, I made 66 Xes. If I did not make it in the morning, I did it later, but I had to get it done each day. I could not stand the idea of not putting that "x" on the chart and ruining the challenge. I knew it was an important decision.

Some days were better than others, but that's ok. The critical part was to sit down with my back straight, become aware of my body in space, breathe in and out consciously and observe my "monkey mind" (an active mind that is hard to settle) with compassion. A storm of thoughts is almost inevitable for most of us. Using the breath to anchor ourselves into the body is a common technique,

It Was Nice To Meet Me Again

but for me, at first, it worked only for a few breaths, then it was boring. I could not keep it up. I found guided meditations or nature sounds worked best to get me out of the storm. The most important thing is to acknowledge the thoughts but let them pass like clouds in the sky. For some, it helps to label the thoughts before letting them go, such as "fear," "worry," "planning," or simply" helpful" or "not helpful." This process allows you to detach from your thoughts. In time, you start noticing a space between thoughts and that is a great feeling.

Meditation is not the absence of thought but freedom from it. You are not your thoughts; you can watch them, investigate them, and see how they make you feel in the body. The best bumper sticker I ever saw is "Don't believe everything you think."

Our thoughts are not to be trusted; they are just our perspectives and they tend to change! Just think about the many times you changed your mind about something or someone. But some of us can use thought to argue forever about anything as if we owned the truth. I grew up in a family with that tendency, and it took a lot of work to "unlearn" the egoic need to be right.

I have to mention that what helped my meditation practice become regular was a free phone application called Insight Timer. It has numerous kinds of meditations with different lengths of time. Whether it's guided by a teacher, filtered by subject or number of minutes, a choice of nature sounds, gentle music, or bells, the choice was mine. It worked for me, and it was great to keep me on track. The app also tells you how many people are meditating with you simultaneously, and that is a powerful international community feeling. You can also thank anyone in the world for meditating with you. Feeling grateful is always "a cherry on top."

This might sound like an advertisement for Insight Timer, but it's not. I'm just grateful that the phone application introduced me to outstanding meditation guides. Some of my favorites are Sarah Blondin, Andrew Johnson, Johnathan Lehman and David Young. Each one has a unique pleasant style and deep insights.

Meditation for Becoming my Own Best Friend
Silvana Graf

Listening to affirmations of self-worth with my hand over my heart was very comforting. Learning to say those affirmations aloud and then hug myself took some work. Thank you for guiding me with your beautiful voice and poetic words Sarah Blondin. At first, it felt very awkward. It's strange how we can say nice things to others and be physically affectionate, but it's difficult to do the same with ourselves. It doesn't have to be that way. We are enough, worthy, and deserve our own unconditional love.

The Insight Timer Meditation Community took me by the hand to meet my complete self again and become my own best friend. There is a journey into our hearts where we can find true peace and love. Our true essence is our spiritual home, always available to us. We are not our habit energy. We are not the negative behavior patterns, fears, anger, and resentment. We need to uncover the trusting, loving being we are; the one that can blend with the universe and feel one with it, in peace. When you find it, in the silence, you will know. You will feel at home and happy.

It's funny how things happen and evolve. What led me to go deeper inside and learn to be my own best friend was the loneliness and separation from a group of twelve friends I often used to socialize with. I went through a period of grief mixed with resentment. There was an eerie silence at the beginning of the lockdown among my group of friends. No one told us that we could not chat more on WhatsApp, talk on the phone, or virtually, however, these friends disappeared as if the Earth had swallowed them. I honestly felt let down. I told myself, "if it's not me organizing the activities with this group, no one reaches out, even online." Maybe I thought I had something I did not; I was sad. I started considering moving away from Ann Arbor and looking for a place that felt more like the countryside. I finally decided it didn't matter anymore if I was further away from Ann Arbor or not. Being close to nature and animals became more important. I learned to live without that group of friends because I became my own favorite friend. I decided that my true friends would find a way to connect.

It Was Nice To Meet Me Again

Fortunately, the steps I took to connect with my true self took me away from resentment and into a world of wonderful and unlimited possibilities. Having expectations of others is always a recipe for suffering. What do we even know about other people's experiences? Maybe what I wanted to receive from my friends was what I was not giving them during that particular time. Maybe everyone was trying to figure out how to navigate these strange times and that is why they were all so quiet in the beginning of the pandemic.

In any case, things happen for a reason. I needed stillness and solitude. I needed to unearth the parts of me that I had neglected. I had spent most of my life molding myself to the different roles that I felt were important. At every junction of my life, I had changed myself for others. The most recent reinvention was becoming a commercial real estate broker in 2016. I wanted to prove to my husband that I could make a significant income. I wanted him to respect me as a professional. Somehow, I never felt like I was enough as I was.

Commercial Real Estate is a fascinating profession and initially, it seemed to fit me like a glove. I am a people person. I love networking. I'm good at negotiations, and my academic foundation in law helped me navigate the world of real estate contracts. I was learning something new and valuable every day. I enjoyed the opportunity for a few years until I realized that it had become a struggle, a source of horrible stress. It is a career that, under the conditions it imposed on me, continuously pushed me to be someone I'm not. I am not competitive. I care more about helping others than making money. This career is also prone to conflicts of interest that I am uncomfortable with. I never felt I fit in that culture. However, I am grateful for everything I learned in the world of commercial real estate brokerage and I consider both of my former managing directors good mentors and friends.

It has become clear that my struggle and stress came because I was not aligned with my true purpose. I will continue working in real estate as a consultant in my own distinct way. I was meant to

Meditation for Becoming my Own Best Friend
Silvana Graf

go through this learning experience for many reasons. I have not wasted any time. I have not closed any doors, and I intend to keep my real estate license active for the foreseeable future.

All I know is that at the moment, I am finally at home being me, rather than struggling to meet other people's expectations and constantly looking for signs of approval. I needed to belong to myself before I could belong anywhere else.

It took a pandemic to find my north and unconditional love. Sarah Blondin taught me to hug myself and not feel weird doing it. Try it. I warn you that embracing yourself for the first time can stir things up. It can make you cry, but they are good cleansing tears. Keep practicing your self-embrace until it feels natural and you feel at home. You deserve your own love. Placing your hand over your heart is also helpful in giving yourself support and confidence. Treat yourself as a newborn baby because you are reborn in every conscious moment and have an infinite number of new starts.

It took a pandemic to understand that being loyal to my inner child is more important than being a recognized professional. Feeding my true self is more important than feeding the ego, which is intertwined with the professional image and worldly achievements. A burden has been lifted to allow my spirit to soar to new heights.

It took a pandemic to learn to embrace the present moment deeply. It sounds easy, but it is not. It takes training to stop the worrying mind from stealing our existence. It takes training to use thinking as a tool to live within our purpose.

Thinking can quickly become a force that takes us away from the heart and into the ego. We must use thinking to support the self, not to undermine it. If you catch yourself ruminating negative thoughts often, your thinking patterns are probably hurting you. Living constantly in the head depletes the heart. On the contrary, practicing meditation is food for the soul. Only in contemplation can you find or rediscover your purpose.

It Was Nice To Meet Me Again

I no longer need to prove myself with accomplishments. I just need to be loving towards myself, others, and nature. Helping others (including animals) is my purpose. I knew that as a young person, but I got lost in trying to prove myself. Fortunately, now I am found, and it was nice to meet my best friend forever – me!

Insights

- Any difficulty in life is an opportunity for growth; find the silver lining.
- Observe your mind and calm it down by meditating regularly.
- Don't believe everything you think, thought is not reality.
- Having expectations of other people sets you up for suffering.
- Solitude is not loneliness; learn to be your best friend.
- When the mind is quiet, you can see clearly; doors open.
- Allow for silence in your life; find your purpose.
- Learn to embrace yourself; you deserve your own love.

Meditation for Becoming my Own Best Friend
Silvana Graf

It Was Nice To Meet Me Again

Photo Credit: Stefan Petrmichl, ashtewan.com

Chapter 3

Meeting Happiness

My husband Rolf built a beautiful bright red bicycle for me, piece by piece. He worked on it for a whole month before Christmas. I had no idea it was for me. I assumed it was one more bike he was building for himself with some new "feature" and that this 4th bike he made would be "the perfect one" for him. Little did I know that it would be the perfect one for me!

One day in mid-May of 2020, I finally put on my helmet, my bike gloves, and off I went with Rolf to test my shiny red bike on West Ellsworth Rd. After riding for a few miles, we stopped to adjust something on my bike. Rolf had been observing my every move and thought my seat was not exactly right. At that moment, a woman probably in her 60's passed by riding her bike. Without a rush in the world, she said, "Isn't this a gorgeous day?" I responded, "It is!" She lifted her roundish, rosy face towards the sun with her hair blowing in the breeze, and she continued her gentle pedaling towards the horizon. "This lady emanates warmth like the sun; this woman is happiness itself; I must follow her," I thought to myself. Rolf finished fixing the seat, and I told him: "I have to follow that woman." I pedaled as fast as I could; I saw she made a turn to the right on Gensley Rd. I was about two blocks away from her, and by the time I turned right, I went up a slope and down and could not see her anymore. She had disappeared, like a dream. I have not been able to forget her. She gave me a clear message: I needed to ride alone without a worry in the world and just be me.

When I narrated the story to my then 90-year-old mother over the phone, she told me, "I know how that woman looked; I can imagine

It Was Nice To Meet Me Again

her, a bit chubby, golden hair, with rosy cheeks and a beautiful smile." Just like she was. My mom and I have telepathy now and then, but this gave me shivers.

My husband is an avid cyclist who exclusively travels on dirt roads. He rides by himself for miles and miles as the hours go by. He has a map in his head of all the scenic dirt roads in western Washtenaw County. He loves exploring and daring himself to go further and further. He has been a good teacher for me in many ways, although it took me many years to understand him, and in some respects, it is still challenging.

I used to resent Rolf's need to ride alone rather than doing it as a family. Occasionally, we did ride together, though. I liked it, but I did not feel secure with rolling hills and had difficulty keeping up. I used to watch my husband and my sons Stefan and Mattias race down the slopes carelessly and thrillingly while I kept my hands tight on the brakes with much fear of falling. The boys would ask me, "What takes you so long? You have gravity working for you!" I had to explain that all my efforts went into slowing down, and I would feel tense because I did not feel safe. In time, by riding alone, without any pressure, I improved my skills and learned to enjoy and feel confident. It did not take long to understand Rolf's passion for riding his bike alone, finally. It is a form of meditation.

During the pandemic, riding my bicycle about 3-4 times a week kept me sane and in the present moment. My country rides became moments of pure joy. I feel free when I ride. Feeling the wind on my face makes me feel alive. It's like being in a dream where you can fly. If I could bottle up this feeling into a jar and apply it every day, I would. My friend, Sandra, suggested that I try to bring that feeling to other aspects of my life. That has been great advice. Just remembering that feeling brightens my day.

When I ride by myself, I can stop to look and take pictures of anything that fascinates me, and there is a lot of that in the countryside. I stop to watch deer approaching cornfields at sunset. I feel a sweet complicity with them. Sorry farmers, I root for the

Meeting Happiness
Silvana Graf

deer to steal a little corn from you. I stop for baby red foxes playing outside an old barn. I stop for wild turkeys, chubby woodchucks, fluffy sheep, a black duck, and baby calves who lick my hand. I also stop for friendly goats, apple-loving horses, and sweet donkeys who always want a snack. How can I not take a picture of birds sitting on power lines like notes on a score? How can I not stop to add to my collection of traditional red barns, rusty and broken structures that show the passage of time? And my favorite: golden bales of straw.

On occasion, I also rode my bike in the country with one or two of my Latin-American girlfriends, which was very nice. It was a safe way to socialize and share my marvelous discoveries. They enjoyed it very much too. I am happy to have opened a new window to the country world for them as well. I feel like Ann Arborites rarely explore the western country roads that are beautiful and close to town.

Worrying and dwelling in the fear of getting sick serves no purpose. It's much better to choose to be mindful and grateful for being alive. During this worldwide epidemic, I chose to meet happiness and freedom on a dirt road, riding mostly by myself.

It Was Nice To Meet Me Again

Insights

- Try something new, preferably outdoors.
- Opportunities appear when you leave your comfort zone.
- Learn to enjoy solitude; it sets you free.
- Show up for your life; explore.
- Be present, have eyes to see and ears to listen.
- Be grateful for life.
- No one can make you happy; you find happiness in yourself.
- When you find it, you can share it with others.

Meeting Happiness
Silvana Graf

It Was Nice To Meet Me Again

Meeting Happiness
Silvana Graf

It Was Nice To Meet Me Again

Chapter 4

Equestrian Love and The Enchanted House on the Hill

One day in the spring of 2020, during one of my country bike rides, I stopped by a horse farm on a hill, next to a beautiful Victorian house. I had always wondered about the lives of the people within. I imagined it being full of elegant antiques.

The following week, during a bike ride with my friend Susana, I showed her the house on the hill and the farm. She told me her daughter had volunteered at an equine therapy center in that same area, and maybe that horse farm that I liked so much was that place. She remembered seeing a picture of a donkey as well, and sure enough, there was an amicable one that would come to the edge of the fence to say hi. That story stayed in my mind. I thought I would enjoy volunteering in a place like that.

So, during another ride that spring, I saw a young man coming out of the side of the beautiful house. He looked at me and asked me if I was lost. I said, "No, I'm not lost, I'm just wandering and wondering... Is this the equine therapy center?"

He replied, "Yes, it is." and then pointed to an arena to the east of the house. "That's where it happens on Wednesdays and Saturdays." "Do you need volunteers?" I asked.

"We can always use more volunteers." and he gave me the website information where I would fill out a form and a phone number to call. I filled out the form and called on a Friday afternoon. A woman answered the phone and asked me a few questions about my experience with horses and why I wanted to volunteer. I explained that I had ridden horses between the ages of 12 and 18. I was not afraid of them and wanted to be in touch with those

It Was Nice To Meet Me Again

beautiful animals again. I also added that I have a soft spot for children with disabilities as my son has Asperger Syndrome (now renamed "high-functioning Autism"). "Ok," she said, "Can you come tomorrow at 8 am?" "Sure," I said. I got up early that Saturday and I went to volunteer.

At the arena, I met Melissa, the instructor. Honestly, she looked like someone I would never approach. Her head was shaved on the sides, she had lots of tattoos, and she was dressed in black. I used to think that style was for angry and hostile people; boy, I learned a lesson from her! Melissa was always friendly to me — she was very knowledgeable about horse therapy and was very good with the kids and teens who came for equine therapy. She knew how to make the horses do what she needed them to do. She was their boss but was caring at the same time.

After a few times on the farm, Melissa encouraged me to get on a horse again. I had not ridden one in 40 years. That moment brought recollections of the insecure teenage me who overcame her fear and got on that horse for the first time. I was so excited. The big difference was that this time, my body immediately remembered a good riding posture, the leg positions, and the way to hold the reins. It was a fantastic feeling; the body has a long-term memory that is beyond thought. I started with just walking and, to my surprise, I remembered how to do the raised trot! My heart raced with excitement; I could not believe I was riding again. It felt wonderful to be up there again, "on top of the world."

That day, I also remembered that I learned "how to fall" in my first riding lesson ever. And, the most important rule is "to get back on that horse right away and keep riding" (unless you are seriously hurt). Fortunately, I did not have to practice that skill this time. I have to say; I never forgot that life lesson. It taught me how to be courageous and resilient.

The following time I rode Apache, I felt braver, and I galloped as well. When you gallop, you follow the horse's rhythm, you get in unison, you are one. It is exhilarating. I felt grateful that Apache let me ride him. He is a great horse, a bit too sensitive to leg prompts though. So, I immediately learned that it was best to give him verbal cues instead of using my legs as I was taught to do when I was a teenager riding horses trained to jump obstacles.

Melissa was proud of me. She said I had a great riding style. Who would have thought I could remember how to ride at age 58! I almost cried with happiness. I thanked her so much for the opportunity.

Getting to know each horse was fun. They were all unique. Every one of them is very well trained and responsive to commands. They had to be; they carried sensitive kids. I think my favorite horse was Tommy. He was surprisingly affectionate. I had never experienced a horse that would lick my hand; it was horse kisses! He would let volunteers comb and braid his amazing blond mane. Tommy is a beautiful Golden Palomino and I hope he is pampered and happy in his new home. Seeing him get in that trailer and leave forever was tough for me.

One of the kids who did the equine therapy was Martin. He was non-verbal autistic but did communicate with some limited sign language. According to his dedicated parents, he had been riding in the program for years as it was beneficial for his well-being.

Melissa had Martin do different exercises and games on the horse for a whole hour while his father and a volunteer like me supported him from the side with a belt with handles. Sometimes I would lead the horse around obstacles, and sometimes, I would hold Martin from the side. One of his exercises involved crossing one arm in front of himself and tapping my hand, like a high five. It was then that he made brief eye contact with me. There was Martin! It felt good to be there for him in that moment when he chose to connect. At the end of the ride, he said thank you by placing a hand on his heart. That gesture somehow felt like a more profound thank you. He reminded me that words are just one form of communication.

I learned so much from Melissa. She knew her stuff, was confident and had a big heart. She helped me reconnect to a part of me that I had abandoned a long time ago. I will always be thankful to her.

It Was Nice To Meet Me Again

The program shut down in the fall of 2020. They sold most of the horses and, in the end, only one horse called Tucker and a donkey called Daisy remained at the farm.

I never stopped going to the farm. I still go, and my heart aches when I don't see my four-legged buddies for a while. My connection to animals has been reignited forever. Nothing makes me happier than spending time in the country with them. I'm back to my roots. My childhood dream of spending time with farm animals as part of my life became a reality starting at 58 years old. It's never too late for a dream to come true. Animals may not talk, but they sure have a lot to communicate, if we listen with love and humility.

When I arrive at the farm, I get a royal welcome. Tucker perks up his ears, nickers, and walks toward me. Daisy raises her head, belts out a hee-haw or some combination of sounds, and approaches me with a determined step. The chickens come running while clucking cutely, and the cats come from different directions to rub against me and cry for attention. I am not much of a cat person, in part because I'm allergic, but these cats won me over. I'm especially fond of the striped one who follows me around even in deep snow. Who could ask for a better welcome party?

The three chickens are all called "Sam". I never called them that out of respect for their individuality. I have to say; those are happy chickens. They roam around freely in beautiful pastures, woods, and, oddly enough, large mounds of dry manure as well. They seem to be fond of those piles of shit. They have two spots where they lay their eggs. I didn't know this before, but you can tell chickens where to lay eggs by just placing a few golf balls in a basket of straw where you want them to nest. They sit on the golf balls until it's time to make some real eggs.

The chickens also have several friends from different species. They especially liked to visit Tommy in his stall, but now that he is gone, they prefer Daisy the donkey. It was adorable to watch them interact. The darker chicken, whom I call "Chicky," likes to ride on Daisy; it's cute. Daisy doesn't mind it, except she occasionally

Equestrian Love and The Enchanted House on the Hill
Silvana Graf

gets pooped on. One of the other chickens chases the cat around, which is funny. Shouldn't it be the other way around?

I have permission to take eggs home if the raccoons don't get to them first. This is a special treat for me as their egg's yolks are bright orange and taste better than any other eggs in the world. Eating those eggs is like ingesting happiness rather than consuming suffering like from inhuman egg mills.

Mike taught me how to feed the animals, and I love it. When there were more horses, each one had a different combination of supplements and cereals. They all got some of this calming food with chamomile. I guess this was a way to keep them calm for the kids with disabilities. I had never heard of animal feed with that on it before, but as a child, chamomile tea was our home remedy for belly aches and any anxiety or sleeplessness.

Feeding the horses hay meant going to the second floor of the West barn, opening a large wooden window, and dropping it down onto the paddock. I thought this was fun! I love the sound of my footsteps on the wooden floors, smelling the hay and old wood. The barn's first floor has beautiful, imperfect stone walls and large wooden beams across the ceiling. There are stalls around the room, each with a plaque that reads the name of its corresponding horse and a photo of said horse. The swallows make nests in crevices of the barn and fly in and out, chirping away, not minding me in the slightest. Being in the barn and the farm makes me feel like a kid. I am living out my childhood dream after all.

A long time ago, Rolf laughed at me when we were driving in the country, and I would open the car's window to smell the air. "I love the smell of horse manure; that smell brings happy memories of my youth," I would say. Nowadays, I get to smell that often. It's funny, the other day I found a picture of a horse on the internet with a label that said, "Happiness has a Smell." It sure does.

Speaking of manure, there was a lot of horse vocabulary I had to learn: "Mucking" stalls and run-ins (which means "shoveling poop") is something I never thought I would do. It has become a rewarding and humbling volunteer activity for me. I never did it as a teen when

It Was Nice To Meet Me Again

I had a horse on the outskirts of Lima. I was too spoiled to do it, and other people were paid to do that job. I am making up for it now. Since the equine therapy stopped, helping with mucking is an excellent excuse to see Tucker and Daisy and give them apples or carrots. After cleaning the stalls, the cherry on top is getting a donkey hug from Daisy. Learning that donkeys give hugs is one of my favorite discoveries from 2020!

I had never been around donkeys and had no idea they were such affectionate beings. If I am feeling down for any reason, I just have to visit Daisy, and she'll give me a tight hug and fix my mood, like magic.

The way the "Daisy hug" happens is that I crouch down and open my arms (come to me gesture); she walks towards me, and she places her head over my shoulder and presses down and inward. It is a lovely hug and long enough to get my endorphins going! The horse therapy might be over, but I get free treatment from Dr. Daisy the Donkey twice a week. I sometimes play soft piano music on my phone and meditate on the first floor of the West barn. Daisy comes and stands next to me as if listening with me.

I loved watching Daisy interact with and relate to other animals. For example, Casey, the mini-horse whom I miss dearly, was best friends with Daisy, and they both liked meditating with me. My heart broke when the owners sold Casey. At least I know she is well-loved where she went; I connected with her new owner on Facebook. On the other hand, Tucker, the horse, is much bigger than Daisy; he upended the pecking order. She was upset and angry for a good while after he arrived. Whenever Tucker approached me for a treat, she would pout by kicking the air and eventually shuffle away in resignation. I think that was the first time I saw the famous patada de burro (donkey kick). Tucker has asserted that he must get his treat first, but while he is busy eating, I run to the other edge of the fence and feed Daisy. Now, I give treats to Daisy while Tucker eats in his stall in the afternoons. Daisy doesn't get an afternoon feeding because she has put on too much weight.

For a while, Daisy looked pregnant, and she had to go on a strict diet. I learned that donkeys have very efficient digestive systems and can gain weight even by grazing too much. Daisy cannot be left out in pastures for very long. I also must be careful not to give her too many carrots or apples which she loves. We must not give in to her enchanting eyes, begging "hee-haw" and head nudges.

The constant challenge at the farm is to keep opossums and raccoons away from the animal feed. When they catch them, unless I rescue them with Mike and take them at least 10 miles away, they get shot by the carpenter. That makes me sad.

The doctor who owns the farm, whom I rarely see, has no idea how his farm changed my life and made a childhood dream come true. I carry out free work, but it's a gift to me, and I'm forever grateful for the opportunity to spend time around his charming animals. Now and then, I run into him, and he thanks me for volunteering and giving attention to the animals.

For the most part, I coordinate animal needs with Mike, the Information Technology expert/animal keeper/midnight gamer and game designer. Mike is a 30-year-old polite and intelligent guy who is open-minded and interested in other cultures (especially the old Icelandic one where women choose their husbands). He learns these things online from international gamers. That is his parallel universe.

Mike has a gentle demeanor in general. He is a similar age to my older son. We are good friends, even though he has to put up with lots of unsolicited motherly advice from me. Once I told him, "I must sound like your mother." He replied that I'm nothing like his mother, and most people like giving him advice, and he is fine and used to it.

At the end of the summer of 2021, Mike adopted seven rabbits from a desperate woman. With much excitement, he built a cage with his own hands and placed them there with food and water. Then he made another cage to separate males from females as they can quickly reproduce after they reach three months of age.

It Was Nice To Meet Me Again

For a while, we didn't know if the females were pregnant since building cages took a little longer than expected. It turned out that at least one of them has four babies now. I hope he can sell them.

Rabbits are adorable and soft. Holding them was a very pleasant and moving experience. My Peruvian friend Cristina, who has eight adopted rabbits, visits the farm with me now and then. She taught me a lot about rabbits. She also rescues dogs. Our love for animals has united us despite our big age difference. Cristina and I met in our dance group "Reflejos Latinos." She is studying medicine at the University of Michigan. I am proud of her. She is a powerful woman with a big heart, always ready to help. Another friend of mine, Gary, donated two rabbit cages which helped a lot. Thankfully, four rabbits were adopted, which means there is only one rabbit per cage. It's a good thing as these are Rex rabbits (I wonder if their name has anything to do with T-Rex). They are massive as adults.

Mike found out on the internet that he can sell rabbit manure at $20/lb. That would help with their maintenance needs (pellets, hay, fresh veggies). He was very generous and gave me a bunch of manure as a thank you gift. It came in handy to fertilize my husband's Peruvian hot pepper plants.

More recently, a shiny black rooster showed up out of nowhere, and Mike got very excited about the new arrival. In a while, there will be chicks running around as well. I learned that people generally don't want more than one rooster, so some drop them off wherever they can or offer them for free. You only need one rooster to mate with many hens. Roosters can be aggressive too. I can attest to that as one day I got close to a hen and the rooster let me know (ouch). It's pleasant to hear him crow and catch the light on his dark plumage. He is handsome indeed.

There's also a shy female black cat that Mike cannot get spayed because she keeps outsmarting everyone. Now she has one kitten, and Mike adopted it immediately. He already has another one from the previous litter of the same cat.

Equestrian Love and The Enchanted House on the Hill
Silvana Graf

I love the animals on the farm. However, I must learn to walk a fine line. They do not belong to me. I need to respect Mike's way of doing things and the owner's decisions about them. I can only help, bring treats and love. I must practice "letting go" of any other urge to control anything. The mom in me always wants to overprotect the animals. Mike keeps reminding me they are tougher than I think.

Dr. Lorraine Smith was the official Physical Therapist and founder of the equine therapy center. I only briefly saw her and spoke to her on the phone once. She had a long struggle with cancer and rarely came out of her house when I volunteered.

I knew Dr. Lorraine wanted the garden island next to the arena weeded, but no volunteer offered to do it, so I did. It was hard but gratifying. Pulling weeds has always been a stress-release activity, but I have to pace myself, or my back will hurt.

The incredible thing was that as I cleared the tall weeds out of the garden island, different objects and sculptures emerged like forgotten treasures of the past. It was fascinating. I found a wooden horse, a stylized cement cat, several wrought iron ornaments, a birdbath, two beautifully sculptured wood mushrooms, and many beautiful plants that deserved to see the light.

When Dr. Lorraine died, the garden project was almost complete. I never knew if she even got to see the progress before she passed away. A few days after she died, I finished embellishing the garden and placed a bright yellow pot of chrysanthemums at the front of it, in her honor.

As can be expected, many weeds came back a year later. Given that I have limited time at the farm, I prefer to keep Daisy and Tucker's space clean for their well-being instead of pulling weeds. In any case, "Some people's weeds are other people's wildflowers." Maybe the "treasures" I unearthed in the garden will be rediscovered with excitement by future people. Some objects will become dust again, like each one of us. Everything is impermanent, and such is life.

It Was Nice To Meet Me Again

What I know about the inside of the "House on the Hill" is that three inhabitants live in the basement, which does have some natural light. The rest of the home is a "construction site" as it's being remodeled. I have only been in a small area of the house for the memorial service for the wife of Dr. Smith last fall. That part was lovely and quaint. I'm still curious about how the rest will turn out to be. But maybe I will never get to see it. The doctor is very private. We don't have a direct channel of communication.

Or...maybe my husband and I could buy the farm someday, but then, we'd probably "chicken out." It's too much responsibility. A farm is a mountain of work, and we are not getting younger! A small ranch on a 1- or 2-acre lot in a country setting, not too far from Ann Arbor, and not too isolated, would be nice and more manageable for our retirement years. It will show up one of these days since now my dreams do come true.

Insights

- Listen to your inner child.
- Fulfilling childhood dreams is possible; be open to possibilities.
- When you volunteer, you receive more than what you give.
- Meeting people that are very "different" from you is an invitation to find our common humanity and develop a compassionate heart.
- The more different a person is from you, the bigger the opportunity to learn.
- Interacting with animals with love and humility makes your heart grow.
- According to the National Institute of Health, interacting with animals has been shown to decrease cortisol levels (stress hormone, lower blood pressure, increase feelings of social support, and boost your mood.
- "Until one has loved an animal, a part of one's soul remains unawakened." – Anatole France

It Was Nice To Meet Me Again

Equestrian Love and The Enchanted House on the Hill
Silvana Graf

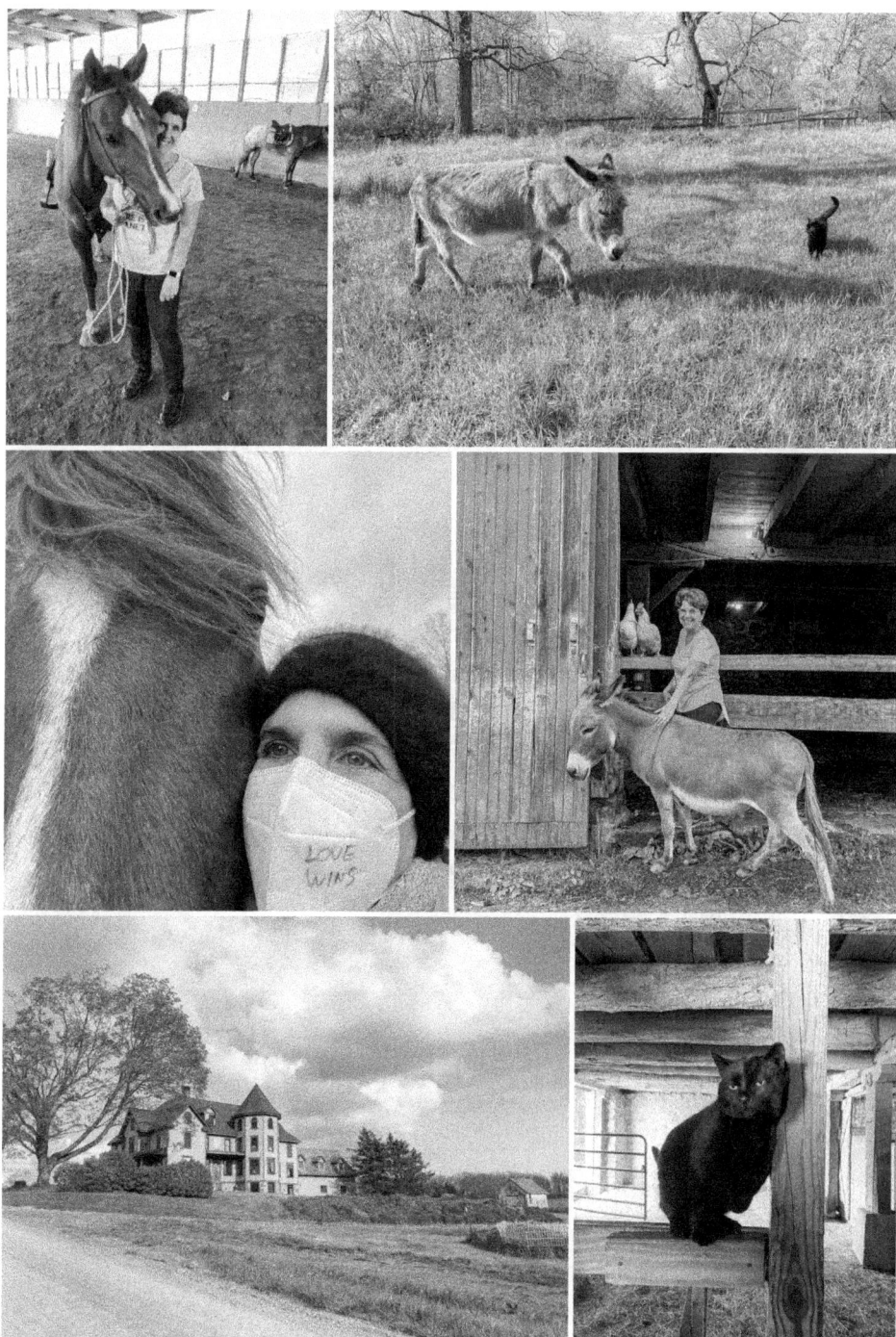

It Was Nice To Meet Me Again

Chapter 5

Finding Yoga Again

My late Aunt Laura first introduced me to yoga when I was about ten years old. At that young age, I used to practice acrobatics and dance. Yoga seemed too slow for me. I liked the challenging poses, but holding them and the slowness drove me a bit nuts. I needed faster movements. I was not ready to take advantage of a yoga teacher in the family. It took many years for me to appreciate the first few lessons my aunt gave me and to realize how yoga shaped her life and helped her through rough times.

La Tía Laurita (Aunt Laurita) was an extraordinary person. She was a serene woman who had long pauses when she spoke. It took some inner work to get used to her silences and not rush in to fill that space. She was a good listener. Many people, including me, would visit her to confide their problems. She had so much love and peace to offer.

My aunt always had little flower vases around the house filled with whatever was blooming in her garden. There was always a touch of warmth among the simple lines of her decor. She had a beautiful garden with a fragrant white jasmine vine over an archway. I had to smell those flowers every time I visited. Her home was an oasis of peace for those who knew her.

My aunt's home did not have much on the walls. She said she liked emptiness, which was the total opposite of my parent's house. My mom filled every space in her own beautiful and exuberant style. She also talked quite a lot with an emphatic voice. It was such a contrast. Now I can tell Zen Buddhism influenced my Tía Laurita.

It Was Nice To Meet Me Again

I remember her mentioning Zen on several occasions during my teen years, but we never had a detailed conversation about it.

Many years later, I spent two or three months in Peru after my wedding in 1988. I was writing my thesis on environmental tort law at her house during the day. Laura's home was the quietest place I knew. At that particular time at her oasis, during our cafecito , I remember discussing the idea of an impersonal God. We had such interesting conversations.

Unfortunately, a few years after I returned to the U.S., my beloved Tía Laura died. She was only 60 years old, and I had no time to ask her many things! That wonderful book of wisdom closed before I had a chance to read it fully. I miss her, although she is with me in different ways. She would be happy to see that my mind finally allows for more extended silences and yoga in my life. I've had an intermittent yoga practice for years, but I intend to make it a regular part of my journey.

During March 2020 and beyond, practicing yoga has helped me feel grounded during uncertain times. I found two excellent teachers online; their names are Jess Timsit and Julia Marie Lopez. I streamed their free classes on our smart TV.

I started with Jess's 30-Day Yoga Challenge; I loved it! She became my familiar mindful yoga friend. I thought no one could be better or more likable than her. Then I started Julia Marie's 30-Day Yoga Challenge, and I loved her too, just as much or more! I liked the power yoga classes. Depending on the day, I still go back to my favorite sessions of different intensities. It's interesting that at the beginning of the pandemic, a time of little opportunity to see my friends, it felt wonderful to have these women in front of me, even if they were recordings on a TV screen. They became my surrogate friends, I guess. There are many talented women-led yoga classes out there. It is empowering.

I am grateful that I found my way back to yoga. It gets my mind anchored in my body and into the present moment. Yoga is indeed a great form of meditation for those like me who have scattered minds. When I practice yoga, it feels like taking a vacation for my ruminating mind. I breathe in and I become the muscles I engage. It's a special time for me.

When practicing yoga, I am patient with my progress and I give thanks for my body's abilities. The outlook for the day changes, especially if I do it in the morning. Positivity envelops my brain. Stretching in the evening has its benefits as well. It's a great way to relax and wind down after the day.

For as little as 20 minutes a day, yoga is life-changing with a pandemic or without.

Insights

- Find the teachers in your life; they might be close.
- Yoga leads you to be in your body in the present moment.
- When your mind is anchored in your body you rest the ruminating mind and a feeling of contentment takes over.
- According to the NIH, research indicates that yoga shifts the balance from a flight-or-fight response to a relaxation response.
- Yoga also lowers blood pressure and increases blood flow to the intestines and vital organs.
- Yoga induces a positive state of mind. Why not try?

It Was Nice To Meet Me Again

Chapter 6

Mindful Thursday Zoom

I have three Peruvian friends who are interested in spirituality. To practice and grow, we had the idea to come together online every other week to discuss interesting readings, podcasts, or YouTube videos on mindfulness or different universal wisdom themes. These meetings have been a wonderful and refreshing experience that began a few months after the pandemic started. Our conversations helped me process the feeling of isolation I had until then.

My mindfulness friends and I have supported each other emotionally through ups and downs. We have encouraged each other to delve into the depths of our souls. We have questioned ingrained limiting beliefs, such as "I am not enough," "I don't deserve," and "Making mistakes is bad." By becoming conscious of these beliefs, we empowered each other to pursue our dreams with courage.

We have explored many teachings drawn from different traditions. The bottom line is that we have increased our mental flexibility, curiosity, and openness to solving any test that life presents to us. We welcome every experience as the teacher we need at this time in our lives. Circumstances are not good or bad; they simply "are," and we are students of life.

We have used several mental tools during our Zoom meetings to observe and question recurring thoughts and the egoic need to control. We have become more aware of when the ego creates stories that cause us suffering. "Pain is inevitable; suffering is optional." (Author Unknown)

It Was Nice To Meet Me Again

In our group, we encourage each other to deal with life's testing experiences head-on, with curiosity, instead of drama. We have become more skilled and nuanced in responding to those around us, especially "the button pushers." We are getting better at placing boundaries from a place of love.

My friends and I have grown together and made brave changes to our lives. We have also been there for each other to embrace our emotional and imperfect humanity and provide compassion and encouragement to continue on the path of awakening our true selves.

My friends are different in their religious beliefs. Sandra V. is agnostic, Rosa Luz, a devout Catholic, and Sandra N. is a student of Buddhism.

Sandra V. leads and facilitates our meetings. She is a scientist who, until recently, worked as a lead researcher in Molecular Genetics and Psychiatry at a prestigious university. She has trained as a facilitator in several personal development methods, including Insight meditation, Bioneuroemoción® (Bioneuroemotion), and follows Alejandra Llamas, the founder of the MMK (Mano Maya Kosha) Institute. Mano Maya Kosha means in Sanskrit, "dissolving the illusory layers of the mind." These methods offer a deeper understanding of the origins of our emotional conflicts. In addition, they provide tools for self-inquiry and development, allowing for a gentle shift in perception. Sandra V. introduced us to Alejandra's podcasts; she and her team have insightful and fun podcasts that we love to discuss. Sandra is honing her skills on her way to becoming a life facilitator. A new career for her. We think she is excellent already.

Rosa Luz studied Pharmacy in Peru; she recently entered the workforce again after a long break being a full-time mother. She volunteers at her Catholic church, helping Hispanic couples with marriage problems and giving communion during Sunday mass. She worked part-time at a pharmacy administering vaccinations and most recently accepted a full-time position as her church's

Mindful Thursday Zoom
Silvana Graf

Hispanic Ministry Coordinator. This job is her dream come true, her true calling. We are profoundly happy for her.

Sandra N. studied Industrial Engineering in Peru; she is a Spanish Language Lecturer at the University of Michigan and has become seriously interested in Buddhism. She practices meditation. Last semester, Sandra N. started teaching a class about racism in Peru. We are proud that she took on the formidable challenge of spotlighting a subject that is often "swept under the rug." She is energized and doing great.

I grew up Catholic; I am a great admirer of Saint Francis of Assisi. In 1986 I found out that I'm half Jewish. That sparked an interest in finding my roots in that tradition as well. I started digging into my family's history, diaspora, and what it looks like today. This predominantly Italian part of my family meets somewhere in the world every four years. Meeting with them has been an incredible journey into my family's Jewish heritage.

When World War II started, one of my relatives was sent to England as a boy to avoid being taken to a concentration camp. Catholic nuns raised him. He didn't know he was Jewish until much later. He is a Catholic priest, and when ordained he chose the name Francis. Coincidentally, my son Stefan has the same middle name and for the same reason. I wanted to honor Francis of Assisi, the humble and compassionate saint who had a special connection with animals.

Many in my extended family adopted whatever the predominant religion was in the area where they moved during or after World War II. My father's family left Trieste, Italy, in 1939; they moved to Argentina first and kept their Jewish heritage private out of fear. They wanted to blend in with Argentinian society, live in peace, and be safe.

In the end, my theory is that the key to peace on Earth is interfaith dialogue. It brings people together and fosters an understanding of the "other." I cannot adhere to any specific religion. I am incapable of accepting any dogmas of faith. For better or for worse, I have a

It Was Nice To Meet Me Again

very pragmatic approach to religion. I adopt practices and rituals that work for me. I've been especially interested in Buddhism for the last 15 years. Their mindfulness techniques are proven methods to calm the mind and achieve contentment.

I have given up belonging to a particular religious group to belong to humanity. As a teenage girl, I used to say, "I don't believe in patriotism; I'm a citizen of the world." Not much has changed regarding this, and the same concept applies to religion.

When my youngest son Mattias was diagnosed with Asperger Syndrome, I was invited to a mindfulness workshop through the Ann Arbor Public Schools for parents of children with disabilities. It was based on a method developed by Jon Kabat-Zinn. Since then, I can say I read almost daily on the subject. Mindfulness helped me immensely in dealing with my son's diagnosis, developing patience in my parenting style, and graceful acceptance. It transformed my life.

In the last 20 years, authors like Jon Kabat-Zinn and Eckhart Tolle explained and taught mindfulness independent of the Buddhist religious aspect. This strategy made the practice more accessible to westerners afraid of committing treason to their religion by practicing Buddhism. There is no reason to tie a life-changing practice to a particular religion. I don't think Buddha would ever mind since he let go of his ego anyway!

When someone asks me if I believe in God, I say, "The answer depends on the definition of God." My idea/feeling of God does not have a religion included. God is not a father figure or someone I can ask favors from. God, to me, is a field of energy, like an ocean, where individual waves (us) manifest for a blip in time. When we die, we blend in again with the One. In the book of my life, we are God, and God is us. I try to live with an open heart and an open mind. I find universal wisdom in most religious traditions that cross my path. Whatever makes me a better, more compassionate person is what I embrace. After all, the religion you grow up with is circumstantial. How can anyone claim to have the truth? If you happen to be born in Japan, you'll likely grow up Buddhist; if in

Spain or Peru, Catholic; if in England, Protestant; if in Pakistan, Muslim. It's a matter of chance for the most part. No one has the absolute truth, and everyone has their truth.

When you think about it, faith is funny. It is always "someone else's gods" that are fiction. However, out of different religious teachings, you can always extract "jewels of wisdom," which is important and beneficial for humankind. Dogmatism, on the contrary, is ego-driven and separates us into believers and non-believers. This element of "otherness" is the root of many wars.

Our Mindful Thursdays are living proof that we can grow together spiritually without exercising dogmatism or trying to convince the other that our truth is "The Truth." Humble "perspectives" or "insights" are what we can honestly claim. In our group, love wins over dogma.

Insights

- Having a small group of friends to talk about mindfulness every other week is a blessing, especially during tough times.
- A team is most helpful to decipher unconscious limiting beliefs.
- Life is neutral but challenging; mindfulness provides tools to deal with life's difficulties head-on.
- Having an open mind is fundamental to learning from others.
- Nobody owns The Truth; we have perspectives.
- Love is more important than dogma.
- Different perspectives enrich life and expand horizons.
- Staying humble is essential to growth.

It Was Nice To Meet Me Again

Chapter 7

Connecting with people far away but Close to my Heart

I have a fantastic community of friends from my childhood in Peru who were very willing to connect through WhatsApp and Zoom during the pandemic. We grew up together from 1st grade until 12th grade. We created a bond during those 12 years; we are like sisters. Despite the distance, we are "one for all and all for one." Always ready to provide needed support in testing times and celebrate virtually each other's successes and birthdays.

The Golden Sis (name of our WhatsApp chat group) have become experts at placing fun festive backgrounds on the application, so it feels like a real party when we celebrate a birthday. WhatsApp is an app that is extremely popular in most parts of the world and now increasingly in the US. We chat, share images, and videos, talk, and see each other's faces for free. Through this application, there are genuinely no borders. Every day we share experiences, helpful information, recipes, and tips on food delivery services. We offer each other help with whatever needs arise.

The Golden Sis and I are turning 60 years old in 2022. We plan a commemorative trip to Greece, Croatia, Spain, and Portugal. Before our travels, we will be learning choreography inspired by the movie "Mamma Mia" (Music from ABBA) to be performed in one of the Greek Islands in July of 2022. I suggested this because I think this preparation will unite us even more and be fun. Dancing is exhilarating, great for the brain, and medicine for the soul. It is the perfect way to get "high" with your natural endorphins. Our training has already started, and we are loving it.

It Was Nice To Meet Me Again

We have already reserved a catamaran for doing "island-hopping" throughout Croatia. I hope our dream becomes a reality and that a new COVID-19 mutation doesn't keep us from doing it. In the worst-case scenario, we can postpone. As with anything we plan these days, we must expect the unexpected and be at peace with it. Such is the river of life.

Connecting with friends from my childhood who know me well helps me nurture my inner child, and I have found out that this is important for my well-being. It is surprising how after our children become adults there's an opening in our lives; a chance to go back to childhood dreams that lay dormant for decades. I am seizing the moment. The fact that I now spend time with animals on a farm, I adopted a dog, and am writing a book is not surprising to my childhood friends, and they are happy for me.

My Peruvian college friends also have a WhatsApp group called "Código 80 Reloaded." 1980 was the year we were admitted to college, and 80 is the number that our college ID cards started with. We connect now and then, virtually as well. This group of friends has a strong bond as well. Our experience at The Catholic University of Peru in the eighties was life-changing for each one of us. We left the pink bubble of our private or parochial schools to venture into a much bigger and more fascinating world. We grew intellectually, and we agree that this period was probably the happiest in our lives. We were young and energetic, and we blossomed in college. We have many beautiful memories to share. Zoom was a great tool to relive our beautiful past together.

On one occasion, my college group organized a live sing-along concert. Our good friend Jorge, who used to play the acoustic guitar for us during college, sang for us songs from the '80s that we knew by hard. Jorge now has a fancy high-tech music studio in his home. It is incredible how one can travel to the past and relive the excitement of being a 20-year-old. We all had a glass of beer or wine in our hands and felt young again!

The pandemic was also a reason to reconnect with my extended family spread around the world. On Saturdays at 11 am, it was fun to participate and learn how things were going in Canada, Germany, Spain, Brazil, Chile, and Peru. We are grateful that no one in our family became seriously ill during the pandemic (so far). Everyone is very responsible and careful.

On Sundays at 1 pm, we had a virtual meeting with my mom, brothers, nieces, and nephews. It was nice to have that unity during the most challenging times of the lockdowns. In some countries, no one could go out the door of their home except to buy food or briefly walk the dog. My niece Andrea, who lives in Madrid, Spain, took turns with her roommates to take the dog out. That dog probably had more walks than ever. People were desperate to get out of their apartments. As things became more flexible with vaccinations, the need for these virtual meetings became less pronounced. The members of my Peruvian family went back to calling my mom individually at their preferred times.

I call my mother almost every day and my dad once or twice a week. I realized early in the pandemic that I had to step up to the plate in the absence of the other social interactions they used to have.

I am now closer to my parents than before COVID-19, especially my mom. I want to talk to her often, and I miss her when I don't. She also keeps me updated on the tumultuous Peruvian political gossip since Marxist-Leninist Pedro Castillo was elected president in July 2021. Populism and extremism have gained positions of power throughout Latin America in the last few years. It's interesting how watching the news helps my mom feel relevant. Many times, I have suggested to her to avoid pessimistic information. After all, she cannot change the problems she hears on TV. But I've come to realize she needs to stay informed and to have a reason to worry. Worrying can be a habit that is hard to kick.

My older brother, Gonzalo, who lives in Peru, told her he does not want to hear her report on the news because it depresses him. In response to that, my mom says her life is limited, she can barely see, and if she doesn't talk about that, what is she going to talk

It Was Nice To Meet Me Again

about? So, when we talk over the phone, I ask her about the latest news, and she feels informed and helpful to me.

In Peru, the shutdowns were a lot stricter than in the U.S. The elderly suffered a great deal from isolation. The vaccine helped significantly; it has been better, but with the newer variants that are more infectious, occasionally crossing over to vaccinated individuals, the older adults are still scared, and much caution needs to be had. Nothing is back to normal in 2022. Masks are still mandatory in Peru. To go inside a store, you need to wear two masks. It is different than in the U.S., where at this point, despite the new variants, face coverings are optional for the "vaccinated," and no one checks if you are vaccinated or not.

My father's routines changed dramatically during the pandemic. He was exceptionally socially active before COVID-19. Socializing has always been the way he cultivates relationships and gets business. He still participates in running his real estate company at the age of 94. The virus slowed his life to a total halt. All he could do was meet online and talk on the phone with people. He lost many pounds from not eating out like he loved to do. This aspect was good for his heart and joint health but not his mood. Before Omicron, there was a window where people from his office who were vaccinated started visiting him now and then, with masks on, which helped him feel relevant, and his mental health improved.

Sometimes I wonder if my dad took this time to do introspection and prepare for the end of his journey. His younger siblings passed away a long time ago. Since I've known him, he has always acted in most respects as if he will live forever. Although when it comes to spending money, it is as if there's no tomorrow! His reasoning will always be a mystery to me regarding that. He did, however, teach me invaluable life lessons. The most important is participating in philanthropy and being a supportive and grateful friend in good times and bad. My father kept our lives interesting by inviting international guests often. I was never excluded from the conversations and learned a lot by listening. I remember having to wear a kimono to welcome a Japanese Toyota executive. His curiosity about the world and everything in it, including different foods was contagious. My mind grew by leaps and bounds every time he took us traveling abroad and on our many road trips through the numerous ecological zones of Peru. My father's colorful life also deserves a whole book.

I talk to my dad over WhatsApp, and I can see him getting frailer and having a harder time retrieving words. Having aging parents far away is tough, but technology and vaccines have helped immensely. After receiving my third vaccine booster shot, I planned another trip to Peru to see my parents. But guess what? The Omicron variant threw another wrench at us, infecting even triple vaccinated individuals! I debated until last minute to go, or to cancel the trip? I chose to postpone my trip to Peru until the Omicron variant wave was on its way out.

Businesses' way to survive everywhere in the world has been to shift to online ordering and door-to-door delivery. I'm glad I can at least surprise my parents with orders of special meals and desserts now and then. They both love that.

Peru is among the countries that will not allow anyone without a COVID-19 vaccine to enter its borders. This type of requirement is not new in the world. I remember traveling with an international vaccination card proving I had the yellow fever vaccine in the eighties, and it is still a requirement to go to most African countries. The card was called "The Yellow Card" (required to prove other vaccinations such as polio and chickenpox). Those were times when vaccinations were not a hot political issue! It's curious that two years into the COVID-19, I don't see the option of getting an international yellow card for COVID-19 vaccinations. I wonder why?

Uncertainty about the virus keeps changing how we can interact with each other. Change is challenging for our nervous system; we crave stability. However, we must stay nimble, and see new situations with curiosity and neutrality rather than drama. A better attitude is to adapt as gracefully as possible.

It Was Nice To Meet Me Again

The river of existence will keep meandering, changing its route slightly or significantly. All we can do is flow with it and "let go of the shore." Shifting my perspective to "expect the unexpected" and find the "silver lining" in any given situation was key to maintaining my sanity. After all, who said life was easy?

Insights

- Connecting and reigniting childhood and college friendships was nurturing and helpful in staying positive during challenging times.

- Calling my elderly parents almost every day helped them throughout the pandemic; it was rewarding for me too.

- Dwelling in gratitude for the lessons learned from the people in my life helped me stay positive.

- Accepting the instability of life and deciding to be flexible and adaptable was fundamental to my mental sanity.

- Resisting change only causes unnecessary suffering; we must flow.

Connecting with people far away but Close to my Heart
Silvana Graf

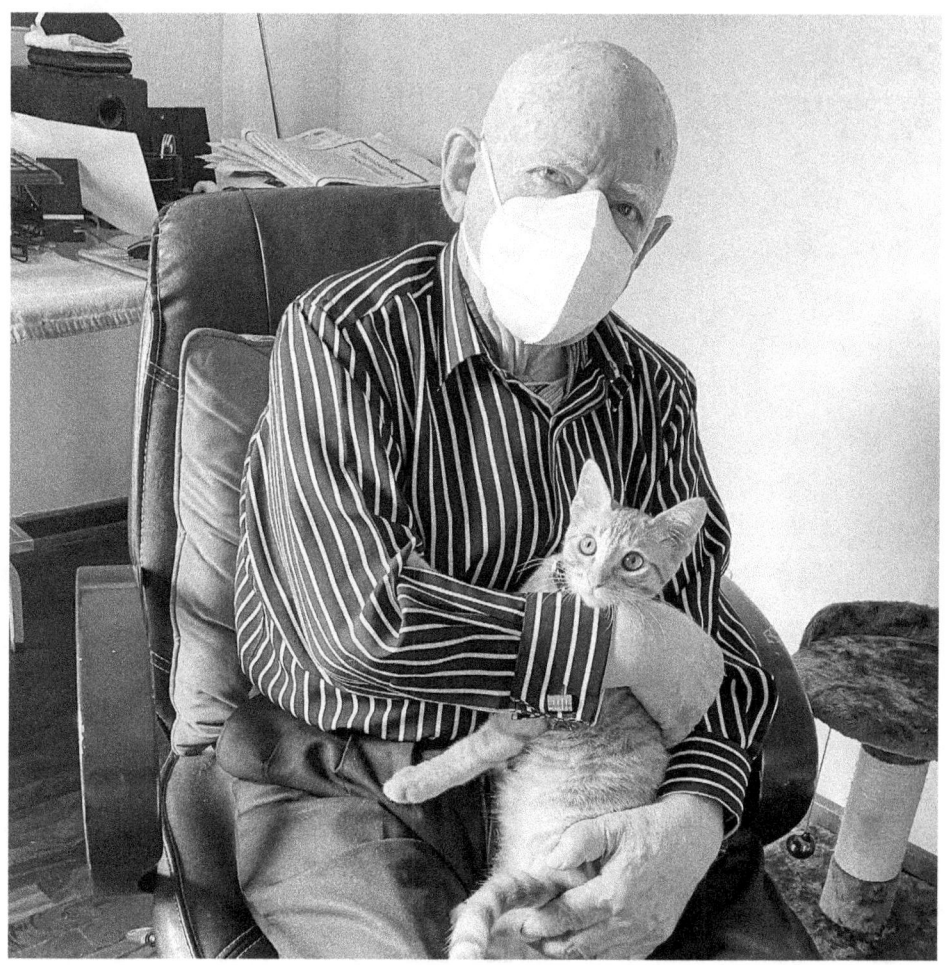

It Was Nice To Meet Me Again

Chapter 8

Lavender Power

Lavender has been my favorite aroma since I was a child. That smell is associated with people I loved as a child, my Tía Laurita and my Nonna Erna (Grandma Erna). As a young girl, people used to tell me that when I dressed up in lavender color my eyes reflected that color slightly. Maybe they imagined things, but it made me feel special. Lavender color is also the light I imagine when doing a body scan meditation. It helps me calm my mind and go to sleep. Most recently, I associate lavender with a small power group of female friends who decided to go smell the flowers in July of 2020.

The first step was creating a WhatsApp group called "Lavender Power." The purpose of the group was to explore lavender farms in southeast Michigan. One summer day, the group masked up, got in my 21-year-old Honda Odyssey van, and journeyed off to the fields.

On our first outing, we visited Nellie's Lavender Estate. The owner is a single mom called Susanne, who makes lovely products with lavender, including a delicious lavender cheesecake and tea, which we got to try out.

Susanne has on her farm the cutest chicken coop I have ever seen. Her chickens are so tame that her beautiful 7-year-old son picks them up and pets them. She has a vegetable cooperative and a wild meadow protected for butterflies and other wildlife. Her neighbors have a few horses, and her mother lives across the field. There is lots of love and attention for that child growing up running in the country, among flowers, birds, and butterflies.

It Was Nice To Meet Me Again

After visiting Susanne's little piece of heaven, we went to visit Devil's Lake–Manitou Beach, where we explored a quaint-artsy little town and found one open restaurant bar. We had a bite to eat and noticed no one wore a mask around there. It was a good thing the place was well ventilated and uncrowded. We are used to Ann Arbor, where most people follow common-sense rules.

It felt great to be doing local tourism in the middle of a pandemic. I think we felt lucky to be able to get out on a friendly expedition like this. We wore masks in the van and only took them off outdoors. Complying with these simple rules meant we could be together safely and enjoy one another's company.

The next lavender expedition was a yoga class in the middle of lavender rows at DeBucks farm on a Saturday morning. Stretching in the gentle morning light surrounded by lavender flowers was an incredible experience. Breathing in the scent of lavender while finding a pose to hold was amazing. Our bodies, our senses, and our minds benefited greatly.

That day, after the class, we visited the honeybee hives at the end of the fields and then proceeded to pick flowers from a forest of sunflowers. Walking among them, we saw many varieties of different sizes and shades of yellow, cream, orange, rust, and burgundy. Some of them were enormous. You could get lost in that sunflower forest. I felt like Alice in Wonderland.

On the third lavender excursion, we dressed in lavender-colored outfits and visited the farm of a young couple on Lavender Lane, Milan. We walked among their rows of lavender plants and bought a few specimens for our gardens. We took cute selfies and enjoyed one another's company again.

I'm happy to report that my lavender plants are thriving in my backyard flower beds. They have attracted beneficial pollinating insects and butterflies. Amazing things happen when you put a plant, a seed, a bulb, or a tree in the soil. With love and care, growth happens. My garden has lots of tiny and great miracles. Gardening is an activity that anyone can do during a pandemic. I certainly chose to plant many "dreams" that resulted in beautiful blooms, fruits, and edible greens.

As far as my Lavender Friends go, each one of them is blooming in different "shades of violet"; they are a lovely bunch. I am grateful to have them in my life and to do fun outdoor activities with them in a small group. These power-women focus on what we CAN do in difficult and uncertain times.

Insights

- Doing local tourism, such as visiting local flower farms can be a pleasant outdoor activity to share with friends during a time when indoor activities are not possible.
- Focusing on smells that bring positive memories and associations is fun and helpful during difficult times.
- Gardening is another activity that is safe and rewarding during a health crisis and any other time.
- Focusing on what you can do instead of dwelling on what you cannot is important to achieving contentment.

It Was Nice To Meet Me Again

Chapter 9

The Forest is my Church

If anyone ever asks my husband and me whether we have a church we attend, we always respond, "Yes, it's the forest!" That is where we practice spirituality, a connection to something larger than ourselves. As a family, we have always enjoyed walking in nature. Our favorite nearby hiking area is the Pinckney Recreation area. The trail is called The Potawatomi. It is a 17.5-mile-long trail, but there are several shorter loops. The woods surround several lakes, and its gently rolling hills make it great for exercise, mountain biking, and scenic views. We never get tired of going there. We feel at peace there, even though we have to make room for fast mountain bikers now and then.

In the spring, it's time for "the frog concert". When they sing, we know this microcosm is fine. Sometimes you can hear two distinct types of songs, and it feels as if they take turns or are talking to each other. Or maybe they have a director telling them when to come in with their part? This free concert happens every spring regardless of any human health crisis.

When I hike, I feel grateful for my legs and the energy that takes over my body. There is something special about feeling the dirt, the roots, and even the rocks under your feet. The forest demands you pay attention, or you'll trip and fall over! When I stop to catch my breath, I look up and feel the embrace of the forest. I see the play of the light sneaking in between the trees while the birds sing and chipmunks shuffle the leaves. And at times it is perfectly quiet and you wonder where the deer, birds, and squirrels are; where have they all gone? What you hear then are your footsteps.

It Was Nice To Meet Me Again

When we walk The Potawatomi in the fall, the changing colors of the leaves make the woods warm and vibrant. There's an additional level of pleasure in the feel and sound of the crunchy leaves under my feet. When you stop, it is also easier to hear which little creature is around you sneaking through the leaves, peaking into the cavity of a fallen log or munching on a walnut. If I'm lucky, I hear or see sandhill cranes flying over or walking at the edge of lakes or patches of wetlands. With their bright red forehead and a wingspan of up to 6 feet, I find them majestic and graceful like those Japanese watercolors you see in art museums. I recently learned they are among the most ancient species of bird. They have been around for at least 10 million years. That makes them even more special to me.

In the depths of winter, our family still goes for walks at the Pinckney Recreation Area. When the lakes are frozen, we can walk on them. If the ice fishers are there, we can safely walk on the surface of the lakes and in the forests that embrace them. It is peaceful and quiet this time of the year. We even record the sounds of cracking ice with our phones. I admit it can be scary, but my husband Rolf is an expert at assessing the thickness and safety of the ice. I trust him without giving up on my own alertness, intuition, and self-responsibility.

Ice will contract and expand with temperature variations. We expect to hear the changes in the ice while walking. When the lake is clear of snow, we see the cracks that happened before and refroze again. This process forms beautiful three-dimensional white "veins" in the lake. Looking carefully, you can see "galaxies" made of air bubbles in the dark ice. They are nature's works of art and an adventure for the imagination.

We look forward to the coldest days of the winter to be able to go walk in our own version of "deep space." With the right shoes and clothes, you can walk in nature in any season. Our best Michigan winters have always been the ones where we walked outdoors the most, regardless of the temperature. Since we cannot change the weather, we embrace it!

The Forest is my Church
Silvana Graf

It is possible to crave the cold. It can make you feel alive and give clarity to the mind. Paying attention to the refreshing feeling on my face when I go outside is a welcomed experience. Correlating the cold to the bright snow perched on every little twig and thistle makes a positive connection in my brain. It is nature's snow art at its best. The more I explore nature in winter, the more I love the cold.

I cannot finish this chapter without writing about Michigan's Upper Peninsula. Every year, our family has a pilgrimage to the area of Pictured Rocks National Lakeshore. I call it a "pilgrimage" because I don't think we have a more spiritual ritual as a family than this one. We have been going there with our boys for about 20 years, and 2021 was no different.

As kids, our sons engraved their initials on a tree on a bluff facing a beautiful inland lake. We could find it for years, until one day it disappeared. This was a gentle reminder of impermanence. It was a birch tree, and naturally, it had shed its skin. But it doesn't matter, because the boys will never forget. It is engraved in their souls.

Every time we go back to hike in the forests of Pictured Rocks, it is like the first time. This place will always surprise us. We feel "awe" and "forever" because it is our spiritual home.

Last fall, we rented a cabin on Lake Powell, near the small town of Munising, in the Pictured Rocks area. Since we were all triple vaccinated, and there was still no news about the Omicron variant, we invited my college friend Pilar from Peru to come along to experience true wilderness and one of the most beautiful lakes in the world, Lake Superior. This was Pilar's first trip since the pandemic started, and I am glad we could share this extraordinary place with her. It was fun to see our familiar paradise through her eyes. Her amazement wouldn't stop.

One day, we hiked to Chapel Beach through the forest (3 miles each way). We went through different forests, deciduous, birch, and

It Was Nice To Meet Me Again

pine. We saw the changing colors of the leaves, different types of colorful mushrooms, bright green carpets of moss followed by white moss that looked like a blanket of clouds as we approached the beach.

After walking for 1.5 hours or so, we arrived at one of the most beautiful lake beaches in the world. White sand, crystal waters, and rock formations with trees perched on top. It is simply breathtaking. We sat on the bluff for some time to suck it all in; once our eyes were full, we had a picnic.

As a family, we have such beautiful memories of this beach. The boys used to play swords with driftwood and jump off the dune. I caught them with my camera in mid-air. We have images of bathing and getting a water massage where the river meets the lake. We have great pictures of their childhood at this magical place. I'm glad Rolf insisted on showing us this far-away place that many Ann Arborites are too lazy or intimidated to visit. It's only an easy 7-hour drive and so worth it.

Pilar is a city person for the most part, but she was looking forward to this adventure. She quickly learned to pay attention to the surface roots of the trees and the possible tripping hazards. After a while, she obtained the experience she needed and caught a perfect rhythm. The forest does that; it fills you with stamina as you discover one treasure after another, and you just want to see more. Then, you belong to the forest.

The colors on Pictured Rocks National Lakeshore result from minerals in the groundwater that ooze and drip on the face of the cliffs. The imagination can run wild. You may see a variety of images on the stone. My fascination is mainly with the beautiful color combinations that this canvas of nature exposes. The rock is a warm light orangey sandstone with iron black, rusty red, white, green, and blue brushstrokes. These natural walls, with the backdrop of the emerald crystal waters of Lake Superior and fall tones of the forest above, are out of this world. There are no

The Forest is my Church
Silvana Graf

words to describe the beauty of this remote corner of our planet. To believe it, one has to experience this from a boat on the lake.

Pilar wanted to tell the whole world about this paradise of pristine waters, pristine forests, and "painted" rock cliffs. She felt very privileged, and so did we. It was especially nice that Stefan, who is now a more avid photographer than me, took many outstanding pictures of this memorable trip to Michigan's Upper Peninsula.

During the pandemic, we have been able to enjoy the forests as usual. We only needed to put our masks on when we saw someone else approaching. It was refreshing to get out there. There is no Covid-19 crisis in nature! Out there, among the trees, everything is normal; the birds still sing; the wind still blows, making the strong but flexible trunks dance gently to its tune. The cottonwood leaves wave "hello" like they always do. The water in the creeks still flows, making its soft trickling music.

What was not normal in the delicate blossoms of spring? What was not right with the deep greens of summer? What was not delightful in the vibrant fiery leaves of the fall? What was not magical in the snowy lace of winter?

We are always free to enjoy the subtle beauty of the forest in every season. In our family's church, there are no worries to be had at the present moment.

It Was Nice To Meet Me Again

Insights

- Whether you go to church or not, nature can be your spiritual place; it will reward your soul with awe and positivity.

- Nature offers beautiful gifts in every season and any weather; it is up to us to open our senses and our hearts to embrace them.

- If you live disconnected from nature you are missing out on the ancestral human experience of belonging to the web of life.

- The pandemic provided an opportunity for many to explore nature like never before. This was a gift to those open to receiving it; it's never late to start.

- You cannot change the weather; so, dress up adequately for it, accept it, and find a way to enjoy the opportunities you have.

- If you cannot get away from the city, a backyard or nearby park has treasures to offer, too.

- Use your eyes to see and your ears to listen attentively.

- To truly enjoy nature, you must be present in body and soul.

- Feel your steps as if you are purposely caressing the Earth.

- Be grateful for your body's abilities to travel in the natural world.

- There is no health crisis in the wild, but magic and seasons to enjoy.

The Forest is my Church
Silvana Graf

Photo Credit: Stefan Petrmichl, ashtewan.com

It Was Nice To Meet Me Again

Photo Credit: Rudolph Petrmichl

Chapter 10

Swimming in the Lake

As my Aunt Laura used to say when I was a young girl, "There is something special about water; you get into it, worries dissolve, and you relax into being." It is true.

By July of 2021, I decided to go back to swimming in my favorite pristine lake. It is in the middle of a state forest. I enjoy going at the end of the day before sunset. Then, the light is perfect, and the water is still warm from absorbing the sun's rays during the day. People who know this "jewel" usually leave for dinner when I arrive. I am sometimes in solitude but never alone.

Swimming at the lake is like returning to the womb of my mother but with a blue sky above. If I swim forward, I see the glimmer on the water's surface and the forests at a distance. I get mesmerized.

If it rains while I swim, it's even more magical to see the drops dancing on the surface of the lake at eye level. The rain is warm in the summer.

If I swim backward, it's like floating in the clouds with the infinite sky above. I don't know anymore if I'm swimming or flying. I feel free, and I move fearlessly without knowing where I'm going. When I stop, I could be anywhere in the lake, but who cares?

It's okay not to have a goal or set direction. At this moment, existing in the water is enough, and it is fulfilling. Why can't we do this more often? Who will give us back the freedom to relax into being except ourselves?

It Was Nice To Meet Me Again

Insights

- Immerse yourself in a body of water, even if it is just your tub; feel your worries dissolve in the water.

- Give yourself permission to just BE.

Chapter 11

The River

In her excellent, eye-opening book *When Things Fall Apart*, Pema Chodron brought to my attention this Hopi Elders' prophecy, delivered in 2000. Digging into this prophecy, with such a fantastic guide, changed my whole perspective on life. Now that I see the complete text of the prophecy, I see there's even more to it. Its relevance is timeless. It is a good exercise to answer the questions posed by the Elders below.

"You have been telling people that this is the Eleventh Hour, now you must go back and tell the people that this is the Hour. And there are things to be considered...

Where are you living?

    What are you doing?

    What are your relationships?

    Are you in the right relationship?

    Where is your water?

Know your garden.

    It is time to speak your truth.

    Create your community.

    Be good to each other.

    And do not look outside yourself for your leader.

Then he clasped his hands together, smiled, and said, "This could be a good time!*

It Was Nice To Meet Me Again

There is a river flowing now very fast. It is so great and swift that there are those who will be afraid. They will try to hold on to the shore. They will feel they are being torn apart and will suffer greatly. Know that the river has its destination. The elders say we must let go of the shore, push off into the middle of the river, keep our eyes open, and our heads above the water.

And I say, see who is in there with you and celebrate. At this time in history, we are to take nothing personally, least of all ourselves. For the moment that we do, our spiritual growth and journey come to a halt.

The time of the lone wolf is over. Gather yourselves! Banish the word 'struggle' from your attitude and your vocabulary. All that we do now must be done in a sacred manner and in celebration.

We are the ones we've been waiting for."

--Hopi Elders' Prophecy, June 8, 2000

Pema Chodron, in her book, focuses on the bold part of the prophecy to give her teachings on facing our fears and accepting the uncertainty of life with courage.

What are the shores I want to hold on to? I often ask myself this question to shine a light on my attachments. I must let go and get used to the fact that my existence is, in essence, uncertain. I need to travel in the middle of the river, expecting the unexpected, facing my fears with courage. To me, this was a counter-intuitive and revolutionary teaching that changed my life forever. The need for stability is imprinted in our DNA. We crave it. We fear change and in that resistance, we create our own suffering in the river of our lives. It is wiser and healthier to be one with the river. We must travel within its current, wherever it goes. Obstacles on the way are meant to teach us, not stop us.

And then, there's the actual river, the Huron. It flows through our town, Ann Arbor. It is a source of wonder and entertainment for those who choose to pay attention to it.

The River
Silvana Graf

I found out a while back that I love kayaking. I have an old van, where my blue plastic kayak fits perfectly inside. I don't need anyone's help getting it in and out of there. This is great as I can decide at the last minute to go on an adventure on the Huron River with my friend Betty who loves to kayak as well. It has been wonderful to explore the Huron River from different points during the pandemic. It was a safe activity to do with friends while chatting and sharing our awe of nature.

It's such a fulfilling joy to admire the white swans that gather near Gallup Park, the family of ducks with the mom and pop at each end of the line of ducklings.

We have "melted" watching a family of Canadian geese waddling up the shore. One baby goose had difficulty climbing, and the whole family stopped; one of the adults went back into the water and guided the gosling towards an easier route. Up they went to follow the others.

We have seen elegant blue herons standing on logs along the edge of the Huron, turtles sunbathing, swans nesting. It is easy to be intimate with nature in this college town if you want to.

One day, we did a group expedition with my friends Betty, Tere, and Perla. We rented kayaks at a canoe livery and went paddling in the Proud Lake Recreation Area in a quiet, narrow, and meandering area of The Huron River. That was special. We navigated very close to a busy beaver and a trusting swan's nest. We stopped by a small dam to have our picnic. While we were eating, we saw a family of geese go out of the river, waddle onto the overpass, and in between humans, perfectly confident. They continued their river journey on the other side of the dam. Yes, at times, Homosapiens can be trusted.

I have to say; it was fun to watch human families having fun in the pool formed by the dam. It seemed for a moment that there was no health crisis.

I think it is refreshing to go into the wilderness; the forest, the river, the birds, and the beavers don't know of any problems with humanity. In that present moment, indeed, there is no virus.

It Was Nice To Meet Me Again

Everyone is okay, alive, enjoying being part of nature and flowing with the river.

Insights

- We must stay present (awake) while traveling in the middle of the river of life.
- Even when life presents hardships, we must deal with obstacles head-on with courage and acceptance.
- "Hanging onto the shore", that is, resisting change will only tear us apart (make us suffer).
- Events in our life are neutral, it's the stories we create in our minds that color reality.
- We must learn the lessons of life as they come, without labeling them as negative. Our job is to find the "silver lining" in any challenge.
- "The River has its destination"; trust life, don't struggle, let go of attachments.
- Let us not be slaves of the "me and mine," of our stuff, our strong opinions, our doctrines; let's be ONE with the river.

The River
Silvana Graf

It Was Nice To Meet Me Again

Chapter 12

Returning to Lake Huron

The last time I had been at Tom and Rosi's house on Lake Huron before COVID-19 struck was for my birthday on August 16, 2019. Going back to Rosi's beach home after almost two years, in July of 2021, felt "out of this world." We had taken so many things for granted in the past. And all of a sudden, our yearly female-bonding summer weekend ritual that started around 2005 disappeared due to the health crisis.

We have innumerable happy memories of quality times spent in Lexington, Michigan. At Tom and Rosi's, we have laughed, sang, danced around a bonfire, kayaked, played in the lake, and even howled at the moon there (yes, we can get pretty crazy).

After receiving two vaccines, Rosi, Betty, Susana A., and I decided to go on a kayaking expedition to Port Austin, one hour north of Rosi's cottage. We reserved our spots on the tour and arrived in Lexington on a Friday night. That way, we could head to Port Austin very early on Saturday morning.

The entire bunch of Latinas could not be there. Still, this small expedition group had a wonderful time savoring again the views of Lake Huron framed by Tom's orange tiger lilies, purple butterfly bushes (with monarchs), daisies with yellow hearts, and the white sand.

Due to strong winds, our kayak expedition was canceled that Saturday morning, but we still went to Port Austin and hired a small motorboat tour instead. Motorboats were allowed to navigate, and we wanted to see Turnip Rock, one way or another. It was a good decision.

It Was Nice To Meet Me Again

Our captain was friendly and knowledgeable. He was able to get us close to the famous Turnip Rock and the small cave behind it. The views were fantastic. We enjoyed the rock cliffs with lush green vegetation on top sprinkled with beautiful homes. A few of the homes have caves developing under them. Nothing is permanent, not even a rock. The waves of lake Huron are persistent and in time the houses will belong to the lake.

We were all exhilarated to have an adventure together again at Lake Huron. As the motorboat gained speed, I felt like those dogs that stick their faces out of the window of a car to feel the air and let their ears flap. It was a sensory pleasure that I had not felt in a while.

Rosi kept thanking us for "stealing her away." It was a break from being a full-time loving grandmother. Usually, she is so dedicated to her grandchildren's activities that she forgets how fun it is to hang out with her adult friends and explore new things.

The rest of the weekend, we walked on the beach at Lexington as if it were the first time. We listened to the sound of the gentle waves as if we were attending the finest concert. We looked and looked at the views filling our eyes, like hungry beings who don't know when the next meal will come and want to make sure their bellies are full. We collected stones and driftwood polished by the mighty Lake Huron. Such treasures, every time, especially this one.

We felt deeply grateful for the opportunity to enjoy this familiar piece of heaven again. We must not take anything or anyone for granted. And one way or another, "the garden of friendship" must be fertilized and watered to keep it blooming.

Returning to Lake Huron
Silvana Graf

Insights

- Reaching out to friends is important to feel connected.
- Friendship must be nurtured and not taken for granted.
- Exploring new and familiar places with friends is very rewarding and helpful to stay positive.

- Planning your social time is as important as planning your exercise and healthy diet according to researchers.
- https://greatergood.berkeley.edu/article/item/how_your_social_life_might_help_you_life_longer

It Was Nice To Meet Me Again

Chapter 13

Adopting Río, The Happy Tripod

During the pandemic, many people adopted pets. Most people were working from home and some were all by themselves. Buying or adopting a pet became popular. The Humane Society became very busy.

In a family of two males that keep to themselves for the most part, and myself, I felt the deep desire to adopt a furry companion with which to cuddle. I grew up with dogs and I love them. It's almost like there's a hole in my heart when I don't have one. I end up having to borrow dogs from my neighbors!

I have two doggie friends that I sometimes walk with and harbor at home when their owners go on vacations, which has not happened in two years. Bo is a gentle Yellow Labrador mix and Toby is a sweet Goldendoodle. With the pandemic, things got complicated, and I was ready to adopt my own dog, but I wanted to make a careful decision.

In the past, I had two dramatically different experiences adopting dogs. One was great and the other one a disaster. I was profoundly happy when I adopted Mac, a 7-year-old Shepard mix. I wondered why on Earth I waited that long to do it. Since moving to the United States, I had been dogless for 20 years. If you wonder why it took so long, my reasoning at the time was that if I had a dog after getting married, all my maternal instincts would go to that being, and I would not want to have kids at all.

So, I had my kids, and they monopolized my attention. There was no room for more, or so I felt. I was hyper-focused on them. Mattias needed special attention due to being on the Autism Spectrum.

It Was Nice To Meet Me Again

After Stefan and Mattias were somewhat independent, I decided to adopt Mac from The Humane Society of the Huron Valley.

I enjoyed Mac for six years, and then he died of old-age complications. It took me two years to recover from his death. In the beginning, my brain would not fully accept that he was no longer with us. I learned there is a scientific explanation for this phenomenon on NPR radio. I could almost hear Mac getting excited in the mornings, which used to happen as soon as he heard activity upstairs. His sounds were ingrained in my brain, so each morning, as I came down the stairs, I expected those sounds and heard them in my head. I would soon remember Mac had died. That sent an electrical shock that felt like a stab in my chest, and I wanted to cry. Only people who have loved an animal as I did can understand what I mean. It is emotional and physical pain. I cried a lot when anything reminded me of him, even watching movies with dogs. It can take a long time to stop crying about losing a pet. I can't imagine what it would be like if one lost a child.

Three years after Mac's passing, I tried adopting a dog again. Cuzco was a beautiful chocolate Labrador-Pitbull mix. He was fun and affectionate with our family, but he became aggressive the minute we walked outside the door. He appeared to want to attack any being that crossed our path. He was powerful. He pulled to get away from me and get to whomever he was targeting. He would pull so hard he would make me trip at times. We tried different trainers, and one of them suggested an electric collar temporarily as a last resort, but nothing would stop him from these scary temper tantrums. I don't know why he was that reactive; maybe he had been trained to fight. There was no way to know how his past life was. Cuzco was a time bomb, and I was not strong enough for him.

After six months of trying different strategies, I had to return Cuzco to the rescue. My son Stefan and I both cried while driving to the rescue. I will never forget the look on his face when we released him in that familiar fenced backyard. He was confused. It took me a long time again to heal from this painful experience. I loved Cuzco despite everything. A part of me still feels like I failed him. If only

Adopting Río, The Happy Tripod
Silvana Graf

I had a fenced yard and lived in the country, I could have kept him, but in my suburban, tidy, family-friendly neighborhood with no fences, all eyes were on him and my family.

Five years later, while listening to my inner voice, I decided to register on www.petfinder.com . I started getting emails featuring adoptable dogs. I looked and read about many adult dogs available for adoption for many months until one little white dog caught my attention from a rescue group called My Chi and Me in Texas. Trio was his name; he only had three legs and had the sweetest face in the world! He is a mix of poodle and Schnauzer. I learned they call that mix a "Schnoodle." He is white as snow, and his ears perk up like two ponytails of the kind toddler girls wear. I applied to adopt him. They reviewed my applications, looked at my home set-up with a video, and then introduced me to Trio over FaceTime. Things went smoothly, and both sides agreed we were "a good match." I was nervous but, at the same time, I knew it was the right thing to do.

As I thought of possible names for my pup, I mentioned "River" to my son Stefan. I explained it was a children's book I found on the internet about a tripod dog by that name. The book's protagonist can do most things any dog can do and is a fun and energetic dog. It was inspiring. Stefan suggested we call him "Río" (River in Spanish), which would be an easy transition from "Trio." It sounds similar. I love his name because I sensed Río would "flow" with our family perfectly, and that is what happened exactly. Ever since Río arrived in our home, my husband and son have been happier and mellower. Rolf says the same about me!

The only story I know about Río's past is that he was found wandering around the streets of Houston badly hurt. As a consequence, his right front leg was amputated on September 23rd, 2021. After that trauma, he had an infection that he overcame. Then finally, he was placed for adoption, and I found my treasure!

My Chi and Me dog rescue has an efficient operation of rehoming excess adoptable dogs from the South of the United States to Michigan. There is high demand for adoptable pets in our area. It's nice to know I live in a place where people care about abandoned

It Was Nice To Meet Me Again

dogs and prefer adopting to buying. The non-profit organization hires large vans like those used at airports (Limos). These vehicles are gutted out to have room for many dog crates. Two drivers take turns driving straight from Houston to Plymouth, Michigan. It is a 19-hour drive with several stops that account for an additional 6 hours for a total of 25 hours of travel time between Houston, Texas, and Plymouth, Michigan.

On Saturday, October 23rd, 2021, I went to a private home in Plymouth that had a long U-shaped driveway. Two vans were parked there, and a line of cars formed to pick up their awaited adoptees. I was impressed by the punctuality and organization of the whole rescue operation. Apparently, some dogs were destined for local Michigan shelters with high adoption rates.

One of the drivers told me that Trio had behaved exceptionally well during the whole trip and was located near the front because of his handicap. The hesitation I had about the long journey for the dogs evaporated as I saw that the dogs had arrived well and in a good mood.

I anxiously waited next to my car, and Río was handed to me like a baby, from the caring driver's arms to mine, a new mama once again. It was incredibly moving to receive my little white angel. My son Mattias drove the car so I could sit with Río on the way home.

My good friend, Tammie, who supports the Detroit Dog Rescue and has five rescues, came to greet Río. She took pictures and videos of my first encounter with Río; they are such beautiful memories now. Tammie gave us many thoughtful gifts to get us started, like when you have a baby! Very generous and unexpected.

I was grateful to be with someone who shared my excitement at that moment. Tammie has a fantastic tripod dog called Eva. She rescued her from the streets of Jordan. Through her, I learned about an internet support community for tripod owners where I could get any needed advice like the type of harness to buy and what to expect from my pup. It's always a good feeling to know other people "in the same boat" who are supportive.

Adopting Río, The Happy Tripod
Silvana Graf

The first helpful tip from the tripod community was, "He will fall on his face now and then but don't be scared; he'll be fine." I'm glad that person said that because it does happen, and I learned to expect it. It helps me that Río doesn't create "a drama" like a person would probably do. He uses his muzzle to prop himself up and keeps going like nothing happened. He insists on peeing like a male dog and balancing on two legs while lifting the third leg, and, in uneven terrain, he sometimes loses balance. Oh, well. Dogs have the advantage of having no "ego" to protect. They live in the moment, solve the problem at hand (at "paw", I should say) and keep going. Instead, a person would probably get embarrassed and start making narratives in the head such as "why do I have a missing leg?", "why me?", "I'm pitiful!", etc., etc.

Río came to remind us that no matter what difficulty we have, we should focus on what we can do. With his attitude, he tells us loud and clear: "Adapt, keep going, don't make stories in your head, and drop the drama, alright."

There is something incredibly delightful about watching a happy and enthusiastic 3-legged dog run every morning, afternoon, and evening with his ears flapping up and down like little wings. It feels as if he will take off any moment into the skies above. It's also notable that he always stops at the creek to listen and watch the water flow no matter how fast he is running. He doesn't miss a bird song, a leaf flying in the wind, or a squirrel running around. If that's not mindfulness, I don't know what is.

I'm not sure if I believe in angels, but if they do exist, Río is one of them. Río inspires me and whomever he meets, and he wants to meet everyone who crosses his path! You look at his eyes, and you see pure love, sweetness embodied. He melts your heart even if you are not a dog person.

I created an Instagram account for him (@riothehappytripaw) to post the beautiful pictures and videos I take of him. Seeing images and videos of Río makes people smile. Photography has been my hobby for many years, and now I have a favorite canine model.

It Was Nice To Meet Me Again

Río has managed to soften my family's rough edges, inspire us, and make our hearts grow. I have never seen my son Mattias care so much for an animal. They are best buddies and roommates. Mattias doesn't even complain about having to dress him for the weather and walk him on the coldest days. It is endearing to see Mattias cuddling with Río. But, I also feel that Río has a mission beyond my family. Río has such an easy-going and calm nature that he can be a therapy dog.

Recently we went together a few times to Glacier Hills Memory Care to accompany and say goodbye to my dear friend Jack. We also gave emotional support to his wife, Ann Holmes, who is a wonderful poet. She has always been an inspiration and was the first person to read my book.

Ann was able to relax while holding and petting Río. At one point, I placed him on the floor, and Río decided to run outside Jack's room and greet elderly ladies in the facility's common area. Río always stays next to me, but he had a higher calling that day, and he brought much happiness to the Glacier Hills community. I will continue to visit with him when possible.

My doggie has much to offer. He is perfect for me despite having only three legs. I love him, and I'm glad I rescued him. Judging by continued posts on social media, you could say I'm "in love" with my dog.

Having a dog was important to me while growing up. I'm glad I went back to my roots again. Río reminds me each day to navigate and flow with the river of life, just like him.

Adopting Río, The Happy Tripod
Silvana Graf

Insights

- A pet can be your teacher if you are open to learning.
- A dog can teach you to be in the present moment.
- A three-legged dog can teach you to let go of your self-pity stories and keep going with a good attitude despite challenges.
- A pet can show you unconditional love and bring out the best in you.
- Drop the drama, be humble, and learn to live with the positivity Río.

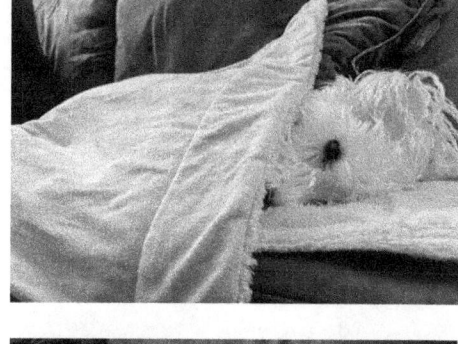

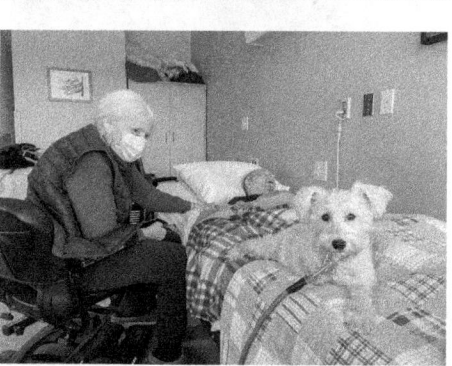

It Was Nice To Meet Me Again

Chapter 14

Rediscovering Music

It's interesting how music is such an important part of our lives starting in our pre-teen years, and throughout our young adulthood. I used to listen to music every day and attended exhilarating live concerts with friends now and then. Music was often a subject of conversations; we bonded through music; we shared it with excitement and generosity.

Music was for daydreaming and letting the imagination go wild. We must have been around 10 years old when I went onto my home's roof with Meche, my friend and next-door neighbor. We had a small cassette player, and as we stared into the night sky, we played Calling Occupants of Interplanetary Craft by The Carpenters, over and over. We hoped that extraterrestrials would want to make contact with us if we focused hard and called them using our minds while playing this song. The lyrics said, "We'd like to make a contact with you, we are your friends." Listening to this song after many years made me cry. We were pure, full of love, and we wanted to spread it throughout the universe. That night, we got to see a couple of flying stars, which we thought could have been UFOs.

As a teen, I spent hours making high-quality recordings of top hits and special musical discoveries for "the next dance party" with my friends. I meticulously cleaned my older brother's vinyl records and carefully recorded them in TDK-II Chrome tapes. I was the lucky one of my friends to get the latest North American and British records. That was thanks to my brother, Gonzalo, who studied in the U.S. and brought them with him to Peru. Because of that privilege, I was

It Was Nice To Meet Me Again

usually the designated DJ for our teenage and later college parties. My neighborhood friends loved to come to our house because we had an entertainment room with awesome speakers and the best and latest music. In that room, we discovered bands such as Supertramp, Pink Floyd, Jethro Tull, Alan Parsons Project, Queen, Stevie Wonder, Captain & Tennille, Fleetwood Mac, Cat Stevens, Carole King, Barbara Streisand, Dire Straits, The Carpenters, Billy Joel, Earth Wind and Fire, Donna Summers, Diana Ross, The Bee Gees and the whole disco phenomenon that made us get off our seats and dance like crazy. Music made us feel alive, and we liked it loud, to feel it in our bones.

I remember times when I was driving to college and listening to my great cassette tapes in the car; the whole world seemed to be walking and moving to the beat of the music I was listening to. On drugs, you might think? Nope, it was my natural music-induced "high."

Then I grew up. I graduated from law school in Peru, got a fellowship to study environmental law and policy at the University of Wisconsin, met Rolf, married, and later became a parent. My kids became the center of my existence, and for some reason, the music went away, far in the background, until it almost disappeared, except for children's music. For years, kid songs, lullabies, and soft classical piano to help my children go to sleep were all I heard. It didn't have to be that way, but it happened like that.

Parenthood forced me to reinvent myself. I placed on hold my dreams to change the world, protect the world from pollution, save the rainforests, fight for animal rights, etc. I left many things that used to be important behind. One of those things was music.

During the pandemic, I had more time to listen to music, which was great. I started remembering the positive effects that music has on me. Music can provide a break from thought; it is felt in the body.

Music is a human primordial language; all cultures have it. Songs tell stories that touch the soul with or without words. Music has the power to transport me back in time to a younger age as if time had never passed. A melody can fill me with emotion, make me cry, give me goosebumps and make me feel an electrical current throughout my body. Music can get me off my chair to dance. It also provides fuel to exercise with fantastic energy. Relaxing music can induce a meditative state or help you go to sleep. Music can be healing. Why did I ever let go of it?

Making an intentional decision to give music a vital place in our lives can make a difference in the quality of our days. There is abundant research showing the health benefits of music and dance. For more details visit these websites: www.hopkinsmedicine.org/health/wellness-and-prevention/keep-your-brain-young-with-music as well as

https://hms.harvard.edu/news-events/publications-archive/brain/dancing-brain

Music can be a good companion while we work, do chores, or it can be our focus. Music inspires and fosters creativity as well. It's okay just to sit and listen or dance like nobody's looking. We don't have to feel guilty about stopping our pursuit of goals to be one with the music, vibrate with it, follow our primordial rhythms and enjoy our present moment. After all, it is what we have.

On the world stage, it was interesting to see how some musicians adapted to new technologies to broadcast music virtually while simultaneously combining their talents with people across the globe. Others sang from their balconies and out of their windows and continued to touch people's hearts like that. Several musicians decided it was a good time to write new music. But for some artists, it was hard not to be in touch with a real audience and they withered in isolation. There are many stories we have not heard yet.

As for myself, in looking for my deepest self, I found my love of music and rhythm again.

It Was Nice To Meet Me Again

Insights

- Giving space for music in our lives is beneficial to our well-being.
- Music can boost creativity and increase motivation and performance.
- If you dance to music, there are added benefits to your brain such as strengthening neural connections, memory, and spatial recognition.
- It can protect mental health and regulate the nervous system.
- Music can improve memory, learning, and cognition.
- Music is known to reduce stress and improve sleep.
- Music therapy has shown improvements in the immune system.
- Music can relieve anxiety and depression.
- Regulate your mood

Chapter 15

Photography of Life

I fell in love with photography when I was a teenager. Being an easily distracted person, especially at that age, I struggled to remember things (Well, I guess I still do). Photography became a way to capture things that I wanted to remember and keep forever.

During the health crisis, I enjoyed taking pictures of the beauty of the countryside. It was an honor to capture, with my phone camera, the Ann Arbor, Dexter, and Chelsea farmlands, to then share them on social media. I fell in love with the rolling dirt roads framed by ever-changing trees, the golden bales of straw that seemingly rolled off a Van Gogh Painting, and the "magic rolling carpets" of black starlings in flight (murmurations). I think I know why the Europeans smuggled those birds into the U.S. in the 19th century. They must have missed their majestic skillful dance in the sky back home. The ugliest-looking black bird has the most beautifully coordinated flight in the world! What a privilege to photograph and film them on West Textile Road.

I am passionate about zooming in on the hearts of flowers and the glitter on the leaves after a freeze. There are no words to perfectly describe a drop of morning dew in an opening tulip or a puff of snow on the magnolia in early spring. The old adage "a picture is worth a thousand words" is true, and that is why I love photography.

I have thoroughly documented the lives of my children with pictures. I am glad I did. It's been a delight to go back to old albums and remember what a beautiful childhood they had. They

It Was Nice To Meet Me Again

will always know they were deeply loved and cared for. They will always know we exposed them to the wilderness since they were babies. We have a photograph of Stefan mesmerized by a creek in the spring of 1992, at two weeks old. Mattias had to wait a little longer. He was born in January, and it was too cold. But that spring of 1997, Rolf took Stefan in a backpack (Stefan got tired walking in the woods) and carried Mattias in a Baby Bjorn front pack. Invaluable memories!

As a photographer, one must find a balance, though. Photography can be a mindfulness teacher that trains your mind to stop and see the details of life, but it can also bring attachment to capturing every possible thing. The need to "keep" can get out of hand. We can easily start seeing our lives through the camera lens instead of living it. I catch myself falling into that trap at times; like the people who cannot stop taking selfies or pictures at parties rather than enjoying the moment and sucking it all in. I find a mindful balance is better.

For example, on November 1st, my dear Mexican friends Teresa and Perla celebrated The Day of the Dead. They made an altar, where we placed images of our close relatives who had passed away and the foods they liked to eat. It was beautiful! Of course, we took beautiful pictures of ourselves together by the altar. But we also stopped and became conscious of the beautiful moment we were sharing. Tere had baked a wonderful "Pan de Muertos ," and my other friends prepared delicious soups and delicacies, including a vegetarian stuffed squash for me (I'm the only vegetarian in the group). We needed to savor each bite carefully.

It had been a long time since we gathered around the table to have a meal. On the Day of the Dead 2021, we did not have knowledge of the Omicron strain of the virus in the U.S. yet, and we were fully vaccinated. My friends and I felt safe having this special meal together. It was a wonderful moment of communion. We felt grateful and truly present for each other.

Pictures are an excellent way to capture the moment. Photography will always be an essential part of my life. When I am older, I will

Photography of Life
Silvana Graf

appreciate even more going through my pictures and reliving moments of the past. Showing up to the present moment with body and mind is essential. I like remembering why a gift is also called "a present."

Insights

- Photography can help you stay present and focus on details.
- It can drive a positive and grateful attitude as you pay attention to the beauty around you.
- It gets you outdoors and exercising.
- It creates meaningful memories.
- Taking pictures promotes sharing and connections with other people.
- Photography as a hobby Improves your creativity and memory.
- It is a form of expression that can boost your self-esteem.
- A photograph speaks directly to the heart.

Photo Credit: Andrea De Romaña

It Was Nice To Meet Me Again

Chapter 16

Befriending Death

Since my teen years, I've been fascinated by death. At that time, my ponderings on death might have been rooted in depression caused by hormonal changes and an analytical mind. I experienced sadness and negativity about the human condition. I saw death as the great escape from the suffering of a sensitive youngster who saw much injustice and cruelty in the world.

During those years, I only saw innocence in animals. I had a special bond with them. I felt misunderstood by the adult world and most of my friends. Somehow, I sounded too "old" for my friends and too young and idealistic for the adults. I would swing from getting lots of energy to save the world to giving up on humanity altogether. I wanted to protect nature from humankind, and it was overwhelming.

When I hear Greta Thunberg (The Swedish Climate Change Teen Activist), I listen to myself at her age. She also sunk into depression before she decided to do something for change. If I would have had access to social media at that age, I could have found twin souls around the world and created a movement like her (maybe), but I was in Lima, Peru, and my peers made fun of my love of nature and worries about pollution. That changed during the end of my college years, and I founded the Peruvian Environmental Law Society with a group of friends. Today, that non-profit organization is a team of 70 professionals and continues to do vital work to protect the environment in Peru. The seed I planted in the '80s grew into a beautiful, strong tree.

It Was Nice To Meet Me Again

As adults, my childhood friends who laughed and even made a clapping game song about "my love for nature," continually remind me how what I said stuck in their heads. Despite not fully understanding its importance at the time, they sincerely thank me for my influence because eventually, "it clicked."

So, after those teen years when I had a mixture of love of life and love of death permeated by sadness, my relationship with death matured into a simple acceptance of the cycle of our existence.

I don't have a problem talking about death. I have had the opportunity to be close to several people who were ill and in their final moments. I was able to speak to them about being at peace with their transition to the end of their journey. I encouraged them to look forward to their freedom from their ailing body.

When I'm close to a dying person, strength comes over me. I remain calm. I want to help, and I believe I can. It's a delicate and scary time for most. I feel people appreciate encouraging words such as, "you are in a transition, but you are going to be ok, don't be afraid." I find the human touch is essential and comforting.

Recently, I could tell that my friend Jack, in his last days, appreciated it when I held his hand. He could not say anything but squeezed my hand back. I would place my hand over his heart and tell him I loved him. When someone seems mostly or totally unresponsive, it is not the time to give up providing emotional support. Playing their favorite music can help, as hearing is the last sense to go.

My father-in-law, Jim, passed away on May 28, 2021. He spent his last week on this Earth at our home surrounded by family. His youngest son, Albert, came from Germany three weeks before his death to be with him. Jim's decline united us as a family, and bringing him to our home was the best decision ever. We gave him love, care, and a nice view out the window. We worked as a team to care for him with the assistance of Arbor Hospice.

What was incredibly surprising to me was that those who avoid talking directly about preparing for death include some doctors!

Befriending Death
Silvana Graf

I knew Jim was dying; he knew it too. We had been struggling to convince him to eat a few bites a day for months, and yet his doctor did not even mention hospice care. Jim also moaned a lot but would tell us he was not in pain. It was frustrating not to be able to help him more with the physical discomfort he felt before he received hospice care.

I had to do research and ask around to find out that hospice care at home is available at the end of life. I learned it's a resource to use even if you are not sure it is the end. People with long-term illnesses can access it too for even a year and get off hospice care if they get better. Why would the doctor not tell us? We could have used the guidance and support a lot earlier than the last week of Jim's life. Nobody talks about it.

At Arbor Hospice, they are experts on death and know the signs and how to properly care for a person at the end of life. The moaning, they explained, was probably pain and discomfort, but Jim could not verbalize it because of his cognitive decline. How would we know? Why didn't the doctor know? Mentioning hospice care is part of the taboo of death in this western society.

What I could not do for Jim is help him have a mindful death. I hope I can do it for myself. I intend to meditate into my death. I hope it is the best meditation into nothingness, into peace itself. "Rest in peace" are the right words, no matter what you believe.

Befriending death and meditating on impermanence helps me show up fully for my life, and for others. If we lived eternally, we would take many things for granted instead of feeling grateful for every moment. Presence is the gift of death if we care to look at her in the eye often.

Like rivers that flow into the sea, even if you don't believe in Heaven, letting go of the ego, ceasing to be, dissolving into nothingness and everythingness, has to be PEACE.

It Was Nice To Meet Me Again

Insights

- Death is part of the cycle of life; speaking freely about preparing for it is healthy.
- Meditating about our inevitable death as part of our lives can help us appreciate every moment.
- If we lived eternally, we would take everything for granted.
- Death can be a friend and teacher to guide us into being present for ourselves and our loved ones.
- Accompanying others in their transition to death is a special goodbye gift.
- Training in meditation can help us die in peace and mindfully some day.
- Accepting death and impermanence helps us not take ourselves so seriously.
- Death will liberate us from our ego and that is peace.

Final Words

In these times of COVID-19, I find no better way to end my book than to say that I believe this virus came to teach us many lessons and it is up to each individual to open up to its teachings.

Nobody said life was easy. But we can choose our attitude when faced with adversity. We can take it as an opportunity for growth, take the plunge into ourselves and get rid of limiting assumptions and beliefs in order to find who we truly are. Hard times are fertile grounds for introspection and growth. It's a slow process, and it takes honest inner work and courage, but the prize is lasting contentment.

Resisting adversity and indulging in thoughts of victimhood causes more suffering and no spiritual growth. We are not our thoughts or the stories we tell ourselves. We have an essential self, where you can rest and draw infinite energy. Accessing that place every day through meditation and mindfulness is a healthy way of living.

Some things may never be the same after this chapter of our lives is over. We must carefully choose what is worth keeping or recovering from our past lives and what is better to let go of permanently. Having that choice is a gift from COVID-19.

During the pandemic of 2020, I went to many places out there and found new connections, but most importantly, in solitude and silence, I found my purpose and my true self.

It was nice to meet me again. Smile. Namaste.

It Was Nice To Meet Me Again

Acknowledgments

Thank you to my friend and poet Ann Holmes for your enthusiasm about my first book and for being the first one to read my manuscript and give me feedback. I also feel fortunate to have Stefan Petrmichl as my eldest son and first editor. It meant a lot to me that you liked my book and appreciated the stories that helped you learn about your roots. I am very grateful to my husband, Rolf, for reading the first few chapters with utmost detail and telling me I was not done with the book. You were right. Your perfectionism will always balance out my need to execute swiftly.

Many thanks to Dennis Pollard, Ph.D., for the great suggestions and for being my final editor. High fives to my marketing team at Persuava, especially Ernesto A. Martínez. You guided me through this new world of book design and publishing.

Special thank you to Sandra Villafuerte for leading our extraordinary mindfulness zoom meetings that encouraged my true self to come out and write a book. Without your help "peeling that onion," it would not have happened. You and our Four Musketeers Group helped me so much through the COVID-19 pandemic and in this rollercoaster called life.

I want to express my deep gratitude to all my wise mindfulness teachers who don't even know me. I need to start with the first one, Jon Kabat-Zinn, then Eckhart Tolle, Pema Chodron, the late Thich

It Was Nice To Meet Me Again

Nhat Hanh, Jack Kornfield, Rick Hanson, Joe Dispenza, and most recently, two amazing women, Alejandra Llamas and Sarah Blondin. The list is even longer. It's been a 15-year journey of transformation that started right after my son's Asperger's diagnosis in 2007. Thank you, Mattias, for coming to this world to be the best teacher of all. I love you so much.

Finally, thank you to all the book characters, some of which don't have their real names to protect their privacy. You all enriched my life and helped me navigate the global health crisis that started in 2020. Let us keep learning and flowing with the river of life together.

Life-Changing Pandemic Insights and Adventures
Silvana Graf

It Was Nice To Meet Me Again
Life-Changing Pandemic Insights and Adventures

Silvana Graf

www.ingramcontent.com/pod-product-compliance
Lightning Source LLC
Chambersburg PA
CBHW060201050426
42446CB00013B/2935